Endorsements

"*I Want It All!*, the testimony of Mark Hyskell, should be that of every genuine follower of Christ in the world. The problem is distinguishing 'all' that is from God, from 'all' that is from other origins, some of which is from the devil. This problem is addressed by Pastor Hyskell with great sincerity, integrity, and knowledge of the Scriptures. Having dealt with these kinds of things for years and having delved deeply into the Holy Scriptures, I believe that this book is not controlled by experience or by preconceived theological conclusions but from the straightforward exegesis of God's Word. This book will help any pastor."

Dr. Paige Patterson
President, Southwestern Baptist Theological Seminary
Fort Worth, Texas

"Mark shares his personal journey of faith relating to the spiritual gift of tongues in an extraordinary and passionate manner. He is intense and thorough. You can relate to his story because his journey happens to many of us. Mark has excellent comments regarding 1 Corinthians chapters 12–14. He does an outstanding job relating how the Holy Spirit works in our lives. You will be glad to follow the journey that Mark has traveled over the years. Thank you, Mark, for sharing."

Dr. Gary Johnson
Executive Director of Missions
Miami Baptist Association, Miami, Florida

ENDORSEMENTS

"*I Want it All!* is a deeply personal and insightful writing of Mark Hyskell's journey through 40 years of ministry. Specifically, he deals with the misconceptions and scriptural truths concerning spiritual gifts. He offers an in-depth scriptural study and practical application for anyone interested or troubled with the big questions of spiritual gifts."

Scott Greenland
President, Cyprus Global, Inc.
International Missions Organization

"Many Bible readers believe that speaking in tongues is a sign of spirituality. This has caused much confusion to the Christian world regarding this spiritual gift. At last, this confusion will be cleared through this book, as the author expounds the issue of tongues in verse-by-verse exposition. I humbly recommend this book to all Bible believers, Bible teachers, and preachers for a personal copy and to make it as one of your best teaching materials in your ministry."

Rey Tabios
Pastor, New Haven Baptist Church
Cagayan de Oro, Philippines

"I have known Mark Hyskell for many years as a friend and as a coworker in Christ's Kingdom work. His book, *I Want It All!* is an account of his extensive study on the subject of spiritual gifts, but it is not written from a comfortable and safe place in a nice church building somewhere. It is an account of his personal journey complete with hardships, discouragements, and difficulties and the raw feelings and emotions these bring. However, with great rejoicing, his journey shows the abundance of God's love and care for us, even when God is all we have. His account is timely, informative, and is an excellent study for any Christian pilgrim who is serious about a committed relationship with God."

Chuck Utsler
Executive Director of Missions
Grady Baptist Association, Chickasha, Oklahoma

"The book is extremely informative and Mark presents the content in an understandable style. It is thought provoking, well presented, and many of the issues [around spiritual gifts] are covered. His thorough presentation of the Scriptures shows that he understands the arguments. This book can help anyone who is dealing with the controversy [of spiritual gifts] in his life and desires to understand the issues [more clearly]."

Danny McCartney
Bible Teacher, Church Leader
Jacksonville, Florida

"The topic of spiritual gifts is in much need of being biblically addressed to prevent many in the kingdom of God from being led astray. Mark Hyskell does just that. Having written from his heart and from the Word, Mark makes it easy for the reader to easily understand our Lord's intentions for the gift(s) that He provides every true follower of Christ. A MUST read!"

Dr. Stephen Peeples
Pastor, Roopville Road Baptist Church
Carrollton, Georgia

I Want It All!

My Journey Through Spiritual Gifts

Mark D. Hyskell

Published by
Innovo Publishing, LLC
www.innovopublishing.com
1-888-546-2111

Providing Full-Service Publishing Services for
Christian Authors, Artists & Organizations: Hardbacks, Paperbacks,
eBooks, Audiobooks, Music & Film

I WANT IT ALL!
My Journey Through Spiritual Gifts
Copyright © 2014 by Mark D. Hyskell
All rights reserved.

Unless otherwise stated, all Scripture is taken from The New King James Version Bible. Copyright © 1997 by Word Publishing, a division of Thomas Nelson, Inc. All rights reserved. Scripture quotations marked (Amp.) are taken from The Amplified Bible. Copyright © 1965 by Zondervan Publishing House. All rights reserved. Scripture quotations marked (NASB) are taken from The New American Standard Bible. Copyright © 1977 by The Lockman Foundation. All rights reserved. Scripture quotations marked (NLT) are taken from The New Living Translation. Copyright © 1996 by Tyndale House Publishers, Inc. All rights reserved. Scripture quotations marked (Amp.), (NASB) are taken from The Comparative Study Bible. Copyright © 1984 by The Zondervan Corporation. All rights reserved.

All poems written by Mark D. Hyskell

No part of this publication may be reproduced, stored in a retrieval system, or transmitted in any form or by any means electronic, mechanical, photocopying, recording, or otherwise, without the prior written permission of the author.

Library of Congress Control Number: 2014949961
ISBN 13: 978-1-61314-245-5

Cover Design & Interior Layout: Innovo Publishing, LLC

Printed in the United States of America
U.S. Printing History

First Edition: October 2014

This book is dedicated to my beloved family. To Gretchen, my wife of forty-one years, who has stood with me through the good, the bad, the ugly and some crazy steps of faith, I am forever grateful. To Mary, Todd, and Rachel Bauer—my daughter, son-in-law, and granddaughter—and to David and April Hyskell, my son and daughter-in-law, I am forever thankful to God for blessing us with such wonderful, loving kids who have become great Christian adults serving the Lord.

Table of Contents

Endorsements 1
Dedication 7
Acknowledgments 11
Preface 13

PART ONE: MY JOURNEY

Chapter 1: The Big Question 19
Chapter 2: The Big Omission 27
Chapter 3: The Big Factor 37

PART TWO: MY STUDY

Chapter 4: The Big Problem 51
Chapter 5: The Big Issue 63
Chapter 6: The Big Priority 85
Chapter 7: The Big Caution 105

PART THREE: MY GIFTS

Chapter 8: The Big Search 139
Chapter 9: The Big Leap 145

Final Note 163
Final Question 167
Scripture References 171
Bibliography 173

Acknowledgments

I would like to acknowledge the help and support of numerous people who have had a part in my life journey in regard to this project. I would like to especially thank Dr. Paige Patterson, president of Southwestern Baptist Theological Seminary, who has not only helped me with the content of this book but has been a great friend and mentor for many years. I would also like to thank my dad, Dr. Joseph F. Hyskell, pastor, missionary, and author for a lifetime of teaching and standing uncompromisingly on God's Word, and my mom, Dixie Hyskell, who has been the greatest prayer warrior in my life. I would like to thank my dear friend Danny McCartney, Th.M, Dallas Theological Seminary for always being ready to dig through scripture with me and help with any project or anything else I need. I want to thank the late Dr. W. A. Criswell, pastor of FBC Dallas, Texas, for being a loving and supportive pastor to me and many others at the Criswell College. I want to acknowledge the invaluable input in my life from the professors and leaders from Luther Rice Seminary, The Criswell College, and Dallas Theological Seminary. I also want to acknowledge the great books from Dr. Paige Patterson, Dr. Spiros Zodhiates, Dr. W. A. Criswell, Dr. John Walvoord, Dr. Roy Zuck, Dr. Warren Wiersbe, Dr. Jerry Vines, Dr. A. T. Robertson, Dr. John MacArthur, and a host of books that have been such helpful resources. I also thank my ministry brothers Gary Johnson, Rey Tabios, Scott Greenland, Chuck Utsler, and Stephen Peeples who have read, given input, and written recommendations for this book. A big thanks to Jennifer Holden for reading the manuscript and offering valuable input. Thank you to all of my young people through the years, and all those I have mentioned in this book, who have been part of my journey. Thank you to all my sons and daughters in ministry who have been a blessing of God. Thank you to each of the church families I have served over these years for your valuable input in my life. Last, but not least, I thank my friends Bart, Darya, Terry, and Yvonne, at Innovo Publishing for graciously answering every question and lending invaluable insight on this project.

Preface

My son, David, who I have always affectionately called "Buddy," was studying scripture and trying to understand more about spiritual gifts. Just as I had heard my dad preach and teach on this issue for years, he had also heard me through his growing-up years. Now as a young man he had a great desire to study and understand it for himself. After he sent me a message asking some provocative questions on the subject, I sensed an urgency in my heart to share some truths from scripture that would shed some light on the subject. The following is my e-mail response to him:

> That is what I want to do. I want to share scripture with you that the Lord used as part of my own journey. Before I get into the scriptures that are generally associated with these issues, in this first section I want to share scriptures the Lord used in my own heart to help begin to answer some of my questions. I am sharing all of this from my heart so you can study the scripture yourself and ask the Holy Spirit to give you direction, not to take it to someone else and ask for their interpretation of these scriptures. Let the Holy Spirit direct you into truth as you study. Learn to listen and hear His voice. You are a man of God, and Jesus said, "when He, the Spirit of truth, has come, He will guide you into all truth" (John 16:13).
>
> I am starting with some of my personal journey concerning the spiritual gifts to help you understand where I came from and how I arrived at my convictions. When I was young, I struggled with scriptural truth on these issues. I heard different things from different people, and it was divisive and confusing. In my heart I wanted to be true to the Lord. I also wanted all that He had in store for me. I desperately cried out to the Lord. I told Him I was willing to go against what I had been taught and make whatever sacrifice was needed to have

everything He wanted me to have and to follow Him completely. My heart was truly open as I told Him, "I want it all!" I wanted any kind of so-called second blessing, baptism, gifts, or anything else as long as it was true to His Word and would honor Him. Even back then, I can remember that was the main criterion in my heart. It had to be true and accurate to His Word. God's Word has always been and still is my rock of absolute truth, though some things seem harder than others to discern and delineate.

I am also sharing these scriptures with the unshakable belief that, *"All Scripture is given by inspiration of God,* and is profitable for doctrine, for reproof, for correction, for instruction in righteousness, *that the man of God may be complete, thoroughly equipped* for every good work (2 Timothy 3:16–17, emphasis added).

As a result of this truth, I am also sharing these scriptures with the belief that a sovereign, omniscient God has never and will never contradict Himself in what He has communicated. Even when it seems there is a contradiction it is always our shortcoming in understanding. We know that our Creator God, Who can literally speak to nothing and make it something, is completely perfect and accurate. Also, the study notes I have included with the scriptures are mostly from resources I did not have back then, but I have included them for your study and help.

There you have it. I have shared with you a personal word that was between my son and me. My heart's desire was to walk through scripture with him. I wanted him to study and pray over scripture and seek the truth from the Holy Spirit of God in his life. I didn't want him to be pressured into believing something because of sweet friends who were charismatic in their orientation or because he heard it from me. I wanted him to study scripture, then pray, and strive to own it himself. That was his heart also.

My journey of struggle, prayer, and study to seek truth from the Holy Spirit is exactly what I have presented in this book. With an open heart before God as a young Christian, I was willing to go against everything I had been taught in conservative theology. I began to devour scripture with a passion and pray that the Holy Spirit would direct me into all truth. I began to discover nuggets of truth in my own personal time with the Lord that excited me. The Holy Spirit began to speak to my heart through certain verses. Different pieces of the puzzle began to come together over several years, and this brief book outlines some of the results.

As I started this journey with my son, I didn't intend to write a book. My goal was to write ten or fifteen pages of scriptural truth he could use to begin his study. As I began to write, the familiar voice of the Holy Spirit within me gave me a desire to keep writing. After that urgency in my soul continued and became more intense, I knew this was meant to be more than a short letter just for us.

I have intentionally tried to write this book in a way that is user friendly and easy to understand. Though I would hope it would be helpful to anyone, it is written for the majority of people who just want to study some related scriptures without all the technical language, complicated arguments, and huge theological words.

I fully understand as I write this that many of my sweet brothers and sisters in Christ will not agree, and that's okay. There are wonderful, sweet Christian people on both sides of this issue. This is in no way an attempt to slam anyone. If that is your intention as you read this book, then your heart is not right before God. It is one thing to try to stand in truth and another thing to stand in truth with a legalistic, vindictive, and unloving attitude. If you do have a desire to read this book, I pray you will receive it in the way I have intended it—as a humble and loving attempt to share my journey and the truths that I feel the Holy Spirit has laid on my heart.

In the first part of this book, I share the beginnings of my own struggle and some of the scriptures that God began to use in my life. In the second part, I share a verse-by-verse commentary of 1 Corinthians chapters 12–14, keeping the context of Paul's writing in view. In the final part, I share some of the crazy stories from critical moments in my own life and how God used them. I pray it will be a blessing.

Heart to Heart

Every morning as I wake up, all life's pressure seems to say
There's no way out, no way over, there's no brighter, fairer day

Then my heart recalls the answer, and I whisper Abba's name
In that moment then I enter where no darkness can remain

Burdens pressing down upon me, questions nagging at my soul
Why the constant pain and pruning, can my heart survive the toll

Then a sweet voice clearly answers, I can carry all your cares
Then I fall into His loving arms, He will always hold me there

Heart to heart with my Father, time stands still beneath His wings
All I need is in those moments, full release my heart He brings

Heart to heart with my Father, in my secret place with Him
All else fades into the background, only love and light stream in.

August 2007

Part 1: My Journey

Chapter 1

The Big Question

Struggling and Praying

Over a period of time, as I sincerely cried out to the Lord for these gifts of which friends had spoken, there was no evidence of any of these things in my own life. There was no work of a "second blessing" or "baptism of the Holy Spirit" manifested by the gift of speaking in tongues as I heard them speak of in such glowing terms. I still wanted it all! I was honestly open and seeking all the Lord had for me even if it would take more time.

As time went on and I didn't see any evidence of these spiritual experiences, this obviously brought up some serious questions in my mind. Why would God have withheld something real that I needed from Him in order to go through all of the conflicts and challenges in my life and ministry? As you know, Buddy, I have faced a good deal of battles and challenges throughout these years of ministry. I had a coven of witches in one ministry location trying to cast spells on me and curse me, even to the point of coming into the church while I was gone from the office and taping a curse on my office door. The Lord would also put me in some situations of having to confront demonic spirits. He would also call me to be ready to risk my life for kingdom work on the mission field. He would take me through severe periods of heartache, such as when you were lost and my heart was dying daily, not to mention these last few years as my deeply beloved mother and prayer warrior has now forgotten who I am with the ravages of Alzheimer's. These, of course, only scratch the surface of forty years of following Christ. Why would my loving heavenly Father withhold from me this wonderful empowerment and gifting with all that He knew I was going to go through in the coming years? It didn't make good sense to me. I needed everything He had for me to serve Him. As I look back over it now, I know my loving heavenly Father would not withhold something I really needed and was genuinely asking for any more than I would send you into a battle without a gun, bullets, or other specific weapons needed to successfully battle the enemy.

Finding Answers

As I was genuinely beginning to search the New Testament scriptures in God's Word, He began to give me answers. I was not just searching the scriptures that my friends referenced, but I was desperately studying all of it for hours a day. I was hurting and needed answers for my own life, not just to prove some theological position. I cried out with tears, "God I need You, and I need all of You every day of my life."

In my diligent search, I finally began to realize that God had already given me all things. The scriptures all through the New Testament began to speak to my heart. "Grace and peace be multiplied to you in the knowledge of God and of Jesus our Lord, as His divine power has *given to us all things that pertain to life and godliness*, through the knowledge of Him who called us by glory and virtue, by which have been *given to us exceedingly great and precious promises*, that through these you may be partakers of the divine nature, having escaped the corruption that is in the world through lust" (2 Peter 1:2–4, emphasis added).

Dr. Kenneth Gangel writes, "All that believers need for spiritual vitality (life) and godly living (*eusebeian*, 'godliness,' 'peity' cf. comments on 1:6, 3:11) is attainable through our knowledge of Him (Christ). An intimate 'full knowledge' (*epignoseos*; cf. 1:2) of Christ is the source of spiritual power and growth . . ." (Walvoord and Zuck 1983, 864). This did not sound at all like I was lacking what I really needed. This sounded like I had been given everything I needed to live a life of godliness and spiritual power in Him.

I also began to realize I had already been baptized in the Holy Spirit. "For as the body is one and has many members, but all the members of that one body, being many, are one body, so also is Christ. For *by one Spirit we were all baptized into one body*—whether Jews or Greeks, whether slaves or free—and *have all been made to drink into one Spirit*" (1 Corinthians 12:12–13, emphasis added).

Dr. David Lowery explains, "The baptism of the Spirit is experienced by all who believe, at the moment of salvation. In that baptism, believers, regardless of nationality (whether Jews or Greeks) or station of life (slave or free), are identified with Christ . . . (baptized . . . into one body) and are indwelt by the Spirit . . . (given the one Spirit to drink)" (Walvoord and Zuck 1983, 533–534).

This did not sound at all like what I had been told I needed by my sweet friends. This clearly told me that by one Spirit we were all baptized into one body. This could not have been any clearer for me. We were all baptized by the same Holy Spirit into one body regardless of who we were. We were all made to drink and partake of the same Holy Spirit.

I also began to realize I have already been blessed with every spiritual blessing. "Blessed be the God and Father of our Lord Jesus Christ, who *HAS blessed us with every spiritual blessing* in the heavenly places in Christ" (Ephesians 1:3, emphasis added).

Buddy, notice the rendering of the Amplified Bible, which is your grandpa's favorite. "Blessing (praise, laudation and eulogy) be to the God and Father of our Lord Jesus Christ, the Messiah, Who has blessed us in Christ with *every spiritual (Holy Spirit given) blessing* in the heavenly realm!" (Ephesians 1:3, Amp., emphasis added).

Dr. Harold Hoehner comments, "'Every spiritual blessing' (*eulogia*) refers to every spiritual enrichment needed for the spiritual life. Since these benefits have already been bestowed on believers, they should not ask for them but rather appropriate them by faith" (Walvoord and Zuck 1983, 616). This did not sound at all like I was lacking the spiritual blessing or empowerment I really needed in Christ. This scripture said He has, past tense, already blessed me with every spiritual blessing, not some.

These truths that God gave me from His Word did not match up with what I had been told by my friends. I was also reminded clearly in scripture that my loving heavenly Father would not withhold from me what is needful when I ask. "If a son asks for bread from any father among you, will he give him a stone? Or if he asks for a fish, will he give him a serpent instead of a fish? Or if he asks for an egg, will he offer him a scorpion? If you then, being evil, know how to give good gifts to your children, *how much more will your heavenly Father give the Holy Spirit* to those who ask Him!" (Luke 11:11–13, emphasis added). My heavenly Father loves me infinitely more than anyone else and would much more than anyone else give me whatever I need as His child who loves and follows Him.

Having been told I was lacking this extra, additional work, I was learning from scripture I was complete in Christ. "For in Him dwells *all the fullness of the Godhead bodily*; and *you are complete in Him*, who is the head of all principality and power" (Colossians 2:9–10, emphasis added). Wow! In Him is all the fullness of the Godhead bodily, and I am complete in Him. What an incredible statement of truth. What an assurance to my heart. This excited me then, and it still excites me now. These scriptural truths were wonderful and undeniable. How could it be that the Bible says I am complete in Him, yet I am not complete in Him according to others?

Dr. John MacArthur said, "Believers are complete in Christ, both positionally by the imputed perfect righteousness of Christ, and the complete sufficiency of all heavenly resources for spiritual maturity" (MacArthur 1997, 1835).

How could it be that one of my first great assurances of scripture, "*I can do all things* through Christ who strengthens me" (Philippians 4:13, emphasis added) was not really accurate? According to what I had been told, I was not prepared to do *all* things and that I still needed this additional work/experience of empowerment and gifting from Him. Philippians has always been one of my favorite books, even from those early days because of the simple truths that I could understand. I truly believed this scripture and remember thinking that just as David faced the giant and overcame him through his faith in God that I could do the same. It made perfect sense to me. God had not changed. He was still all powerful, and He was still looking for those who would put their simple, teenager kind of faith in Him and walk forward in His power. I remember wanting that to be me, though I had no clue what giants I would face in the future.

How could it be that Jesus said, ". . . when He, the Spirit of truth, has come, He will *guide you into all truth*" (John 16:13, emphasis added), and yet I seemed unable to grasp this incredibly important truth I was told about? I was genuinely seeking this guidance from the Holy Spirit and ready to follow His guidance wherever that led me. This scripture spoke of guiding into ALL truth. Not part of it, not fragments of it, not even most of it, but into all of it. So in my young mind and simple faith in God that is what I held to. He would guide me into "all truth," especially the most important enabling, empowering, gifting kind of truth.

The only conclusions that could make any sense were either 1) God was withholding something from me that was a special empowerment and gifting that I needed, 2) I was somehow spiritually retarded/dense and could not grasp the truth, 3) I was really unwilling to see and grasp the truth, or 4) God was withholding it until a later time. Knowing how loving my heavenly Father is, I know the first was not true. Though the second was a possibility, it seemed to make no sense in light of the scripture that the Holy Spirit would lead me into all truth. Others might think the third was true concerning the Holy Spirit's gifting, empowering, and enabling, but I was genuinely seeking. Even accepting the fourth as a possibility, forty years of seeking and walking closely with the Lord and being guided by the Holy Spirit into all kinds of spiritually challenging and confrontational situations and battles, it is *untenable*, which is defined as, "not able to be defended" (Woolf 1981, 1274).

Buddy, as I was studying God's Word through all those early years, the conflict of these differing beliefs seemed to make no sense to me and didn't seem to line up with the overview of scripture and the other clear truths I was discovering. This same disconnect with scripture is what has driven others away from the charismatic movement. For instance, George Gardiner didn't want all the arguments he had been taught; he simply wanted an answer to the question, what does the Bible say? He writes, "It was this question, following the disillusionment common to Charismatics, which drove me out of the movement and into the relief and freedom I enjoy today. It all began with nagging questions about the gulf between Charismatic practices and Scriptural statements—a very wide gulf!" (Gardiner 1974, 8). I can tell you that now after walking with the Lord for forty years, preaching and teaching God's Word for over thirty years, along with undergraduate and graduate degrees and fourteen years on the mission field, it still doesn't make sense to me with the overview of scripture.

Now, I understand when I am weak and heartbroken and don't know how to pray, God has given me His answer. "Likewise the Spirit also helps in our weaknesses. For we do not know what we should pray for as we ought, but the *Spirit Himself makes intercession for us with groanings which cannot be uttered*. Now He who searches the hearts knows what the mind of the Spirit is, *because He makes intercession for the saints according to the will of God*" (Romans 8:26, emphasis added).

This is what I have desperately depended on in the deepest, darkest times of my life. He knows my heart. He knows that hurt. He knows the discouragement. He knows when I am at the end of my rope. Why would I need some kind of unknown prayer language when His Word has told me that He looks at my heart, hears my deepest needs, and intercedes for exactly what I need with communications in the Godhead that I could never understand anyway? The bottom line is He intercedes for me in the perfect way when I am beyond human words to really express what is in my heart. It truly leaves me without any need that the Holy Spirit cannot fully understand, interpret the deepest needs of my life, and then communicate them perfectly to the Father, which is the fullest expression of everything needed within my life. What more could I ever need or want?

I have also depended heavily many times on a scripture in Philippians. "And my *God shall supply all your need* according to His riches in glory by Christ Jesus" (Philippians 4:19, emphasis added). I fully understand the contextual interpretation here concerning the gift that was sent and how God would reciprocate, but I also believe there is a spiritual application. I believe from the overview of scripture, and even some of the scriptures I just used, that God has clearly promised to meet all our spiritual needs as He said, "I have been blessed with every spiritual blessing" (Ephesians 1:3, paraphrased). How can that be if I am still lacking something that is spiritually, critically important to my life and ministry? In reality, if there really is this extra, additional experience of empowerment and gifting they speak of, then God really has not met all my needs. I will proclaim loudly and clearly that God has met all my needs all these years as a minister and missionary both physically and spiritually and in every other way. There is one miraculous story after another of God's great provision that would fill a large book. And I believe there is no way of counting all of the things God has done for me and my family that I don't even know about.

Another scripture struck my heart many years ago. "Now this is the confidence that we have in Him, that if we *ask anything according to His will*, He hears us. And if we know that He hears us, whatever we ask, *we know that we have the petitions that we have asked of Him*" (1 John 5:14–15, emphasis added). This is the clincher that answers the big question of this chapter. What a wonderful assurance from God! If I ask anything that is specifically according to His will for my life, then I can know without a doubt I will have what I asked of Him. How could there be anything more in God's will for my life than having the full complement of God's enabling power and gifting to serve Him and complete what He has called me to do? Without question, this is God's will for my life, and I have genuinely asked for it and believe He has given it. To say God has not done this in my life would be the equivalent of saying this scripture is not true. He clearly has done it and answered my prayers in amazing ways through this journey of life, and He continues to do it, especially through the mission work to which He has called me.

Buddy, this is a very brief overview of some of the questions and study I was going through as I struggled with the subject of spiritual gifts. I thought this would be helpful for you to understand my journey and why many of these things seemed to make no sense. Though I definitely have a fuller understanding of the history, grammar, and primary interpretation of these scriptures from the writer to the recipients after all these years, it has not significantly changed my convictions concerning these issues. As a matter of fact, the more I have learned the more the Lord has solidified the truths of His Word concerning these issues. Actually, it has been a sweet blessing from the Lord to go over these things once again, and He has spoken to my heart in a fresh way. While I have a desire to continue this chapter with many more scriptures that illustrate this point, I am trusting that these will reveal the truth I realized. In this first section, I have not dealt with any of the foundational understanding, the associated problems, the background of the culture of that time, or the classic scriptures themselves because I just wanted to share from my heart to my son. I didn't want to just start throwing books at you but wanted you to hear from me. You want to study God's Word, and that is what I was doing. So, here is a very brief few lines of what the Lord was doing in my life. I pray that the Lord uses His Word to be a blessing to you also. Love you, Daddy.

My Son

The King is coming I heard them sing
Their voices loud with joy did ring
But in my eyes the tears did form
And in my heart a raging storm

My Son the one I love so much
Was filled with doubts and fears and such
Unsure that he would fly away
To heaven's bright, eternal day

My soul bows down, I cannot rest
The fear explodes within my breast
I cry to God please touch his heart
Without him I cannot depart

And then one night the call it came
My soul distraught and casting blame
He shared through tears your mighty touch
Had changed his heart the change was such

That joy did leap within my soul
My son is safe, my son is whole
The King is coming now I sing
My voice with joy to heaven did ring.

2006

Chapter 2

The Big Omission

How Could This Be Missing?

I called the first chapter "The Big Question: Why would God withhold something so critically important to my life and ministry?" This chapter I am calling "The Big Omission: Why would God omit something so critically important to my life and ministry from scripture?" To *omit* is defined as "to leave out or leave unmentioned" (Woolf 1981, 794).

Though I understand that an argument from silence is not the strongest argument, in this instance I believe it is legitimate and a point worthy of consideration, especially when we consider what is omitted in scripture concerning this issue. To me, it is astounding what is omitted in reference to the Holy Spirit and His work in our lives when I consider what some believe about a later baptism of the Holy Spirit.

We have numerous commands and exhortations from scripture concerning the Holy Spirit in our lives. Let's look at just a few.

Be Filled with the Spirit

We are exhorted to be filled with the Spirit. "Therefore do not be unwise, but understand what the will of the Lord is. And do not be drunk with wine, in which is dissipation; *but be filled with the Spirit*" (Ephesians 5:17–18, emphasis added).

So what does this really mean to be filled with the Spirit? Dr. Hoehner explains, ". . . Thus in this relationship, as a believer is yielded to the Lord and controlled by Him, he increasingly manifests the fruit of the Spirit (Gal. 5:22–23). The Spirit's indwelling (John 7:37–39, 14:17; Rom. 5:5, 8:9; 1 Cor. 2:12, 6:19–20; 1 John 3:24, 4:13), sealing (2 Cor. 1:22; Eph. 1:13, 4:30), and baptism (1 Cor. 12:13; Gal. 3:27) occur at the time of regeneration and thus are not commanded. However, believers are commanded to be filled constantly with the Holy Spirit. Each Christian has all the Spirit, but the command here is that the Spirit have all of him" (Walvoord and Zuck 1983, 640). Dr. Witty shares the essence of this filling with a story about the great evangelist Dwight L. Moody. "Two men were discussing the ministry of Dwight L. Moody. One said, 'To me the secret of Dwight L. Moody's power is this: He has the Holy Spirit.' 'I do not agree,' replied the other, 'for to me the secret of Dwight L. Moody's power is that the Holy Ghost has him'" (Witty 1966, 61).

So, our actions and behaviors can be controlled by the intoxicating effect of wine, which leads to debauchery. Dr. Hoehner comments on the original word: "the word *asotia* is translated debauchery (NIV, RSV), 'excess' (KJV), 'riot' (ASV), and 'dissipation' (NASB). All these give the idea of profligate or licentious living that is wasteful" (Walvoord and Zuck 1983, 640).

Our lives can be controlled by the inner working of the Holy Spirit of God within the lives of believers who are yielded to His control and watching Him carry out His supernatural purposes. This produces a life well lived and invested for the kingdom. The Criswell Study Bible states, "The filling of the Spirit is an absolute control of the believer's life when that life is yielded to Christ. Special fillings occur in times of need for particular spiritual prowess. The 'filling' is to be distinguished from the 'baptism' of the Holy Spirit, the latter being a once for all transaction at the moment of salvation (cf. 1 Cor. 12:13, note)" (Criswell 1979, 1389).

Dr. Paige Patterson states, "Believers are commanded to be 'filled' with the Spirit (Eph. 5:18), but they are never told to be 'baptized' with the Spirit" (Patterson 1983, 219). This is one of the keys to understanding the Holy Spirit's work in our lives and also to understanding the confusion surrounding it. We are commanded to be filled with the Holy Spirit but never commanded to be baptized in the Holy Spirit. This wonderful filling spoken of in Ephesians 5:18 is the ongoing experience while the baptism is the once-for-all experience. The filling is to be the ongoing experience of life while the baptism is the glorious possession completed at regeneration. The English Standard Version Study Bible comments on this filling, "The command in Greek (*plerousthe*) is a present imperative and does not describe a onetime 'filling' but a regular pattern of life" (Dennis 2008, 2271). The "filling" is ongoing while the "baptism" is completed at conversion.

The interesting corollary truth to the life that is filled/controlled by the Holy Spirit is that the filled/controlled life will most certainly manifest the fruit of the Spirit. That will be a hallmark or proof of the life that is filled/controlled by the Holy Spirit as sure as an apple tree will produce apples. "But the fruit of the Spirit is love, joy, peace, long-suffering, kindness, goodness, faithfulness, gentleness, self-control" (Galatians 5:22–23). This is the fruit of the Holy Spirit! This is what He produces in and through the life of one who is yielded to Him. These are the characteristics of the life of one who is filled with the Holy Spirit.

Walk in the Spirit

We are told to "walk" in the Spirit in Galatians 5:16. "I say then: *Walk in the Spirit*, and you shall not fulfill the lust of the flesh" (Galatians 5:16, emphasis added).

So what does this really mean to walk in the Spirit? Albert Barnes breaks it down this way, ". . . This is the true rule about overcoming the propensities of your carnal natures, and of avoiding the evils of strife and contention. Walk . . . the Christian life is often represented as a journey, and the word walk, in the scripture, is often equivalent to live . . . if we live under the influences of that Spirit, we need not fear the power of the sensual and corrupt propensities of our nature" (Barnes 1965, 383).

In reference to the original language here, Dr. Donald Campbell explains, "the verb *peripateite* is a present imperative and is literally translated, 'keep on walking'" (Walvoord and Zuck 1983, 607).

In order to not fulfill the lust of the flesh, we are to live our lives under the influences/control of the Holy Spirit of God Who lives within us. This is an imperative in our lives that is to be an ongoing, consistent lifestyle. We cannot live this way if we are living a life that is controlled by the flesh. We can only live this way as the Holy Spirit of God is directing and controlling us and our hearts are yielded to Him. When we walk in the Spirit by His empowerment within us, we watch Him accomplish His supernatural purposes through our lives.

Take the Sword of the Spirit

We are told to take the sword of the Spirit in Ephesians 6:17. "And take the helmet of salvation, and the sword of the Spirit, which is the word of God" (Ephesians 6:17).

So what does this really mean to take the sword of the Spirit? Dr. MacArthur comments, "As the sword was the soldier's only weapon, so God's Word is the only needed weapon, infinitely more powerful than any of Satan's. The Greek term refers to a small weapon (6-18 in. long). It was used both defensively to fend off Satan's attacks, and offensively to help destroy the enemy's strategies. It is the truth of Scripture" (MacArthur 1997, 1815).

Ephesians 6 is the classic passage about putting on the whole armor of God. Each of the pieces of armor are mentioned and finally the sword. To take this sword of the Spirit is to use the Holy Spirit-inspired, powerful truths of the Word of God to defeat the darkness and lies of the enemy. We use the light of God's Word to dispel the darkness of the enemy. We speak the truth of God's Word to overcome the enemy's lies. We proclaim the truth from God's Word about our lives to defeat the lies from the enemy. We stand in the truth of God's Word about who we are in Christ against the lies of the enemy about who he says we are. We speak the truth. We study the truth. We memorize the truth. We speak the truth of God's Word that, "'I can do all things through Christ who strengthens me' (Philippians 4:13) against the lies of the enemy who tells me I am too weak and continues to try and convince me I am unable to accomplish much of anything." We speak the truth of God's Word that, "There is therefore now no condemnation to those who are in Christ Jesus, who do not walk according to the flesh, but according to the Spirit" (Romans 8:1)—against the lies of the enemy that we are condemned and just playing a game. We swing the Sword of the Spirit that says, "And you, being dead in your trespasses and the uncircumcision of your flesh, He has made alive together with Him, having forgiven you all trespasses, having wiped out the hand writing of requirements that was against us, which was contrary to us. And He has taken it out of the way, having nailed it to the cross" (Colossians 2:13–14)—against the lies of the enemy that we are not forgiven and are filthy, no-good sinners. We pray the truth. We live the truth. We are in a battle so we must always have our swords ready. We take the sword of the Spirit, which is God's Word, and slash and destroy the lies, the darkness, the attacks, the accusations, and everything else thrown against us meant to steal, to kill, and to destroy.

Putting These Pieces Together

With these truths in mind, one could also legitimately ask, how could you successfully be filled with the Spirit, walk in the Spirit, and take the sword of the Spirit as we are all called on to do, without the essential empowerment and gifting of the Holy Spirit through the baptism in the Holy Spirit? Remember, to be filled with the Spirit as we saw in these verses is to be living a life that is controlled by the Holy Spirit of God. In addition, to walk in the Spirit as we saw in these verses is to be living a life under the influences/control of the Holy Spirit of God. Finally, to take the sword of the Spirit as we saw in these verses is to be fighting a spiritual battle with a spiritual weapon under the direction and with the supernatural power of the Holy Spirit of God.

Of all the commands and exhortations we have in scripture concerning the Holy Spirit in our lives, we are never commanded or exhorted to be or seek to be baptized in the Holy Spirit sometime after salvation. This is an amazing omission considering the importance of this event. If as some of our sweet friends believe, this baptism of the Holy Spirit occurs sometime after salvation and is the source of critically important empowerment and gifting to serve the Lord, then it would be one of the highest priorities, if not the very first thing we would be exhorted to seek in scripture. With this in mind, one would think that many times and in many ways the scripture would give us clear direction in this critical matter. However, there is not one instance of scripture telling/exhorting/commanding us to be baptized in the Spirit, or to be seeking to be baptized in the Spirit sometime after salvation. How could that possibly be?

What we do see in Acts chapter 1 as Jesus is speaking to these first generation believers about the coming "promise" of the Father is for them to simply "wait." "And being assembled together with them, He commanded them not to depart from Jerusalem, but to *wait for the Promise of the Father*, which, He said, you have heard from Me; for John truly baptized with water, but you shall be baptized with the Holy Spirit not many days from now" (Acts 1:4–5, emphasis added).

This actually happened around ten days later. Jesus promised them many times that after He left, God would send the Holy Spirit of promise. "Behold, *I send the Promise* of my Father upon you; but tarry in the city of Jerusalem until you are endued with power from on high" (Luke 24:49, emphasis added). And also in John, ". . . If anyone thirsts, let him come to Me and drink. He who believes in Me, as the Scripture has said, out of his heart will flow rivers of living water. But this He spoke concerning the Spirit, *whom those believing in Him WOULD receive*; for the Holy Spirit was not yet given, because Jesus was not yet glorified" (John 7:37–39, emphasis added).

At this pivotal point in history, transitioning from the Old Covenant to the New Covenant, the Holy Spirit had not yet been given in this way, so the apostles had to wait for this promise to be fulfilled at the Day of Pentecost. His command is for them to simply "wait" for this sovereign promise that was to come for the first time in the new era according to God's design and timing. That is why they had to wait in this unique situation.

The Holy Spirit would now come to permanently indwell believers for the very first time in this transition period. In the Old Testament, the Holy Spirit would come upon people for a period of time for a special mission or purpose but never permanently. This then was a unique time, as there could be only one time the Holy Spirit would come in this "new way" to indwell believers forever. After this unique, short transitional period from the Old Covenant to the New Covenant in Christ, with the Holy Spirit coming to indwell believers permanently for the first time, along with the Gentiles experiencing the same transitional event in Acts 8:14–17, 10:44–46, 19:6, this "waiting" is never seen again in scripture. It is confirmed that these events in Acts are the same, unique Pentecost experiences with the Gentiles when Peter says, ". . . Men and brethren, you know that a good while ago God chose among us, that by my mouth the Gentiles should hear the word of the gospel and believe. So God, who knows the heart, acknowledged them *by giving them the Holy Spirit, just as He did to us, and made no distinction between us and them*, purifying their hearts by faith" (Acts 15:7–9, emphasis added).

This is the famous Jerusalem Council where the apostles and elders had met specifically to discuss the inclusion of the Gentiles into the Body of Christ. There had been a dispute about what to require of the Gentiles who were becoming part of this new Body of Christ. Peter made it clear that these Gentiles had been baptized in the Holy Spirit just as the apostles had been and that God had made no distinction between them. After this glorious beginning of the church at Pentecost, this "waiting" on the baptism of the Holy Spirit is never recorded again.

So what is the reason for this great omission? The other New Testament book in which we see the baptism of the Holy Spirit mentioned is 1 Corinthians where we have this clear statement, *"For by one Spirit we were all baptized into one body*—whether Jews or Greeks, whether slaves or free—and have *all been made to drink into one Spirit"* (1 Corinthians 12:13, emphasis added).

The infant church had begun with the inclusion of Jews and Gentiles being baptized, empowered, and supernaturally authenticated in the same way. The apostles were overseeing each of these instances in Acts under the direction of the Holy Spirit to bring Jews, Gentiles, and Samaritans into unity within the one new Body of Christ.

They are told to wait and when the promised Holy Spirit comes to indwell them, Jesus said, "But *you shall receive power when the Holy Spirit has come upon you,* and *you shall be witnesses* to Me in Jerusalem, and in all Judea and Samaria, and to the end of the earth" (Acts 1:8, emphasis added).

Then some days later when this promise came to pass, scripture records, "And suddenly there came a sound from heaven, as of a rushing mighty wind, and it filled the whole house where they were sitting. Then there appeared to them divided tongues, as of fire, and one sat upon each of them. And *they were all filled with the Holy Spirit* and began to speak with other tongues, as the Spirit gave them utterance" (Acts 2:2–4, emphasis added).

Now that the Holy Spirit had come to live within them permanently, they were empowered by God to be instruments revealing His supernatural power. Now, the Holy Spirit would be in them forever as is seen when Jesus said, "And I will pray the Father, and He will give you another Helper, that He may *abide with you forever*—the Spirit of truth, whom the world cannot receive, because it neither sees Him nor knows Him; but you know Him, for He dwells with you, *and will be in you"* (John 14:16–17, emphasis added).

It is interesting to note that in the critically important issues for the believer, such as putting on the whole armor of God in Ephesians 6, we see very distinct and intense language used. In verse 16 we are told, "*above all*, taking the shield of faith with which you will be able to quench all the fiery darts of the wicked one" (Ephesians 6:16, emphasis added).

It is also interesting to note that there are no "above all" kind of statements or language used concerning our seeking to be baptized in the Holy Spirit after salvation. Such as, "Above all make sure that you pray/seek to be baptized in the Holy Spirit after salvation." This naturally brings up the big question why. With something that many claim to be the greatest empowering and gifting experience in the life of the believer, with accompanying supernatural abilities, why would there be no command, no exhortation, or instruction from the Holy Spirit Himself who inspired scripture?

Let's now answer the big question of this chapter. There was no command, exhortation, or instruction from the Holy Spirit in inspired scripture to be baptized in the Spirit after salvation because of the truth that we have already seen in 1 Corinthians 12:13. "For *by one Spirit we were all baptized into one body*—whether Jews or Greeks, whether slaves or free—and have *all been made to drink into one Spirit*" (1 Corinthians 12:13, emphasis added).

Dr. Patterson explains, "The apostle continued by explaining precisely how a man becomes a part of the body of Christ. The Holy Spirit immersed each one into the body of Christ. Only this critically important verse lucidly explains what is meant by the 'baptism of the Holy Spirit.' The expression itself is found seven times in the Bible. Most of these occur in the Gospels and generally represent the prophecy of John the Baptist that the one coming after him would baptize 'with the Holy Ghost, and with fire' (Matt. 3:11)" (Patterson 1983, 217).

In his rather long discussion and dissection of this verse, Dr. Patterson finally concludes after looking at the various possibilities, "At the moment of conversion the Holy Spirit immerses every believer into the body of Jesus Christ" (Patterson 1983, 219).

Dr. Warren Wiersbe also comments on this verse and explains, "The baptism of the Spirit occurs at conversion when the Spirit enters the believing sinner, gives him new life, and makes his body the temple of God. All believers have experienced this once-for-all baptism (12:13). Nowhere does the Scripture command us to seek this baptism, because we have already experienced it and it need not be repeated" (Wiersbe 1985, 126). Gardiner says, "I could not find one command anywhere in the New Testament for Christians to seek the baptism of the Holy Spirit. Instead, I discovered (as outlined in the section on first Corinthians 12) that the 'baptism' had occurred when I was placed in the body of Christ at my conversion" (Gardiner 1974, 9).

Since this initial coming of the Holy Spirit at Pentecost to start this new era, all believers in Christ are baptized in the Holy Spirit at the moment of spiritual regeneration/salvation. He comes to indwell us permanently and make us new creatures in Christ. "Therefore, if anyone is in Christ, *he is a new creation*; old things have passed away; behold, all things have become new" (2 Corinthians 5:17, emphasis added).

We are new creations because of what the Holy Spirit has done within us. In addition, we see in scripture, "But you are not in the flesh but in the Spirit, *if indeed the Spirit of God dwells in you. Now if anyone does not have the Spirit of Christ, he is not His*" (Romans 8:9, emphasis added).

The indwelling of the Holy Spirit is something that has already taken place in the life of believers when they are baptized in the Holy Spirit at the time of regeneration. Dr. Walvoord comments, "One of the prevailing misconceptions of the baptism of the Holy Spirit is the notion that it is a special ministration enjoyed by only a few Christians. On the contrary, the Scriptures make it plain that every Christian is baptized by the Holy Spirit at the moment of salvation" (Walvoord 1958, 139). There is no "later" baptism because, according to scripture, there has already been a baptism. There is no second or third work as it relates to the baptism of the Holy Spirit and the resulting empowerment and gifts that He brings because it has already occurred when I was made into a new creature in Christ.

Buddy, I want to be clear about my heart attitude as I share all this. Is it possible to disagree with brothers and sisters in Christ and not love them less? Absolutely! I believe that Jesus has given us clear instructions concerning that love in the book of John. "A new commandment I give to you, that you love one another; as I have loved you, that you also love one another. By this all will know that you are My disciples, if you have love for one another" (John 13:34–35).

Also, love just happens to be the first segment of the fruit of the Holy Spirit, Who dwells within us as shown in Galatians 5:22. I have no desire to get into heated debates that end up with hurt feelings and wedges being driven between us. I am simply sharing what I see in scripture for you and my other kids in ministry who may be interested to see it. This is absolutely no diatribe railing against people who have different views. Most of the people I have known within what I call the charismatic community have been some of the sweetest people I have seen. This is not a diatribe, but rather a humble sharing of my time in scripture over the years. I feel that I would be letting you down as the father that God has placed in your life to not share what I see in scripture.

Drowning in Grace

I'm fully enriched, I'm fully embraced
I'm loved beyond words, I'm drowning in grace
Each path I have walked with heartache and pain
I see now was paved and meant for my gain.

The failures I've felt, the storms I have feared
Though crushing at times with sickness and tears
Were never allowed to separate me
From His loving hand, from His plan for me

As older I grow, more clearly I see
The paths, the pains, the storms, the seas
Were grace in disguise, a loving embrace
I'm loved beyond words, I'm drowning in grace.

May 2014

Chapter 3
The Big Factor

Truth

Buddy, you have mentioned numerous times how sincere our dear Christian friends are concerning their beliefs and practices. So, let's consider this factor in light of what we are studying.

If *sincere* means genuinely believing what you believe is the truth, I believe they are very sincere. I do really love them and the sweet spirit of Christ they project. The indispensable key element here is *truth*. Truth is the "Big Factor." Truth is not truth just because you believe it to be truth and call it truth. If that is all there is to it, then you yourself become the ultimate definer of truth. That is the view of the secular world when they make the statement, "that is your truth." By that definition, everyone can claim they have truth even when they have diametrically opposing views. We see many examples in our world of people claiming something is true even when it is what God has said is not true. Truth is absolute. We have the absolute standard of truth from God Himself contained in His Word. Therefore, whatever we claim to be truth must be what God has said is truth, not just what we might believe to be true.

Sincerity

This brings up the more thorny issue of two people believing different things, and both of them claiming they have God's truth from His Word. I believe there are sincere Christian people who believe you can lose your salvation. They have scriptures they passionately use to try to prove their point and claim they have God's truth from His Word. I believe there are sincere Christian people who believe women should never wear pants, never cut their hair, and that it is a sin for men to have long hair. They have scriptures they passionately use to try to prove their point and claim they have God's truth from His Word. I believe there are sincere Christian people who believe they are supposed to handle poisonous snakes in their services (they better be very sincere), in order to show the protective power of God. They have scriptures they use with great fervor to try to prove their point and claim they have God's truth from His Word. There may also be sincere Christian people who believe they can be baptized for the dead. They actually use scripture right out of 1 Corinthians (15:29) that we are studying to prove their point and claim they have God's truth from His Word. I'm sure you get the point here.

Extreme Sincerity

Further, to see the true, extreme capacity for error with sincerity, we look to the Middle East. With our working definition of sincere—truly believing what they believe is true—we are shocked by the sincerity of those who strap bombs around their bodies and truly believe it is God's will for them to murder as many infidels as possible while blowing their own bodies into little pieces.

I was shocked to watch a TV show the other day about Rev. Moon and The Unification Church. Numerous church members were calling him the Messiah, and when he and his wife walked out on the stage they played, "The Hallelujah Chorus." He claims to be the Messiah and tens of thousands believe him. The human capacity to believe something is true when in reality it is not true is mind-boggling.

Bizarre Sincerity

You and I do not believe those beliefs are actually true and accurate to God's Word. I have run into people who truly, passionately believe some of these and many other things to be truth from God's Word. As you may remember, Buddy, I have had some bizarre experiences through the years. In one church, our secretary came into my office with a very alarmed look on her face. She told me there were some weird guys who had come into the church and wanted to talk to someone. So I went to find them and invited them to my office. These guys had long robes, long beards, and were barefoot. They called themselves the "Christ Brothers." They sat down and we began to discuss some scripture. During that discussion, they found out that I eat meat. Immediately, they recoiled in horror and told me I was like a murderer. I asked how they came to that conclusion, and they pointed me to, "He who kills a bull is as if he slays a man" (Isaiah 66:3).

That was it! That was all they used! That was all they had! They had completely misused this scripture. This scripture was contrasting true and false worship and heart motives and had nothing to do with what they claimed. However, they were sincere by our definition here. Shortly after that, I noticed one of them pull out a rolling paper from his satchel and begin to put some green stuff in it. Having grown up in the 60s and 70s, I had a good idea of what he was doing. When I asked him, "What in the world are you doing rolling a joint in my office?" his response was, "It's just God's green herbs, man!" At that point, I asked them to get out of my office and got up from my desk to help them out. As they began to get up, they also told me Jesus had already come back. I said, "Have you actually seen Him?" "They said they had seen Him and knew where He was. I rather harshly responded, "That's funny because Matthew says, 'For as the lightning comes from the east and flashes to the west, so also will the coming of the Son of Man be' (Matthew 24:27) and I haven't seen it!" This further enraged them, and they both walked out the door with the last one yelling a few expletives, including God's damnation on me and slamming my door so hard it made a cracking sound. Granted this is an extreme example, but it does illustrate the point.

They will passionately go to scripture and try to defend their "truth" position. They will use verses that do address their particular belief in one way or another. They are convinced of their position, and in many instances would claim the Holy Spirit revealed this to them.

I have actually heard someone say, "There could not possibly be only one way to heaven!" She believed that was truth. She also claimed that she was a Christian. However, when we look at the absolute standard of truth, which is God's Word, it says, "Jesus said to him, I am the way, the truth, and the life. *No one comes* to the Father *except through Me*" (John 14:6, emphasis added).

God's Word, our absolute standard of truth, says the exact opposite of what she said. Jesus said very clearly and definitively there is only one way to heaven. She passionately defended her position and was sincere in her belief of it. In other words, she truly believed what she was saying was true. Though these are pretty extreme examples, it does make the point that someone can be very passionate and sincere and still be incorrect. In fact, they can be sweet, loving, giving people and still be incorrect.

When a belief based on passion, emotion, and experience becomes the dominating factor (even though that fact may be vigorously denied) we are in danger. So the real point becomes not sincerity, not passion, but accuracy. I believe this is seen in Paul's letter to Timothy. "Study and be eager and do your utmost to present yourself to God approved (tested by trial), a workman who has no cause to be ashamed, correctly analyzing and accurately dividing—[rightly handling and skillfully teaching]—the Word of Truth" (2 Timothy 2:15, Amp.).

Here is where the rubber meets the road. I will grant you up front that our dear friends believe they have "rightly divided" the Word of Truth. However, probably most of these people I have mentioned, if not all of them, would claim the same. They believe they have it right. So it is up to us to study diligently and "rightly divide" the truth under the direction of the Holy Spirit Who will, "lead us into all truth."

Buddy, though this is sometimes a difficult thing with people we love, we can never afford to just agree and go with the flow. We cannot afford to just follow sincerity and passion. We cannot just accept something as true because we admire someone and appreciate his or her spirit. We must dig in the mine of God's Word for ourselves and find the real gold instead of something that sparkles like it. We must love them and also love God's Word and strive to "rightly divide" it. As we begin this diligent search together with prayerful dependence on the direction of the Holy Spirit, I believe He will guide us into all truth.

Context

I believe many of these inaccurate scriptural beliefs just mentioned, along with many others, could be avoided with a few "interpretation principles."

Each of these illustrations has a common thread. They have isolated a verse or verses and removed them from the full context around them. Many times, as the "Christ Brothers" did, they remove it from the context of the paragraph, chapter, book, and the whole Bible. They then viewed it outside of the proper context the Holy Spirit inspired to be written. This is a dangerous practice when it comes to biblical interpretation and hermeneutical (the study of biblical interpretation) principles. That is why you have heard me speak so often of the critical importance of "context." It has been said by some that you could take an isolated phrase of scripture, completely divorce it from its context, and prove almost any belief. Whether that is literally true I don't know, but I have certainly seen many people try.

One of the most glaring examples of removing a scripture from its context is currently being used by the secular world almost as a fad. It is, "you shall know the truth, and the truth shall set you free." I have called it a "hijacked truth." It is a wonderful truth of scripture that, with its proper context, takes the student to a God-ordained, accurate destination of understanding. Without its God-ordained context, the truth is hijacked and ultimately leads the student to whatever premise is being espoused by the user.

This wonderful truth from Jesus viewed with its God-ordained context adds the accurate overview for a genuine understanding. The Bible says, "Then Jesus said to those Jews who believed Him, 'If you abide in My word, you are My disciples indeed. And you shall know the truth, and the truth shall make you free'" (John 8:31–32).

This true meaning is radically different from the way most people are using it. Within its God-ordained context, there is a conditional statement. Jesus said, "IF you abide in My word, you shall know the truth, and the truth shall make you free" (John 8:31–32, paraphrased). Needless to say, most people using this phrase know nothing of abiding in His Word. They are simply using a phrase that sounds good but is completely divorced from its full meaning, completely superficial, and hijacked from its original intent.

This dangerous lack of a proper context is illustrated by a humorous story that pastors tell. It goes something like this. There was a Christian who desperately needed answers from the Lord. He prayed and asked the Lord to speak to him from the Word. He asked the Lord for an answer about what he needed to do in his life. With his eyes closed, he opened his Bible and placed his finger down on a verse, and as he opened his eyes, they fell upon the phrase, "Then he threw down the pieces of silver in the temple and departed, and went and hanged himself" (Matthew 27:5).

Knowing that couldn't be right, he tried again. He closed his eyes, opened his Bible, and placed his finger down on another verse, and as he opened his eyes, he saw the phrase, "Then Jesus said to him, 'Go and do likewise'" (Luke 10:37).

Though this is a silly illustration, it does, to some degree, show the danger of taking a phrase, a verse, or verses and completely removing them from the proper context. The Holy Spirit of God inspired all of scripture with a sovereignly given context. This becomes all the more amazing when you understand the array of human authors who were used and the many centuries that separated them. The context of scripture was given by the Holy Spirit of God. To ignore that context is to ignore the Holy Spirit's sovereign direction and misuse His Word.

Scripture Doesn't Contradict Scripture

Another of these principles of interpretation is that God will not ever contradict Himself in His Word. When we have one passage of scripture that seems to contradict another passage of scripture, we must understand that the Holy Spirit of God, Who inspired all scripture, has not contradicted Himself.

Therefore, in the case of someone claiming that God's Word has contradicted itself contrasting one passage with another, it is simply his or her lack of understanding in one facet or another. An omniscient God certainly does not contradict Himself, and the Omnipotent One is certainly capable of preserving His Word from human corruption.

In the case of someone claiming an interpretation of scripture does actually contradict another passage or passages of scripture, that person's interpretation is inaccurate. To claim an interpretation of scripture that contradicts other scriptures and the context of scripture shows their lack of understanding in one facet or another. It does not necessarily show any kind of ill intent or motive, but it does reveal a lack of understanding. No matter how passionately it is defended, it does not change the truth of the sovereign unity of scripture.

Scripture Interprets Scripture

Another of these interpretation principles that works together with the previous two is that scripture interprets scripture. In other words, various scripture passages help shed light on and interpret other scripture passages. Sometimes when we have a scripture passage that seems more obscure, other scripture passages that may be more obvious will shed light on and help interpret the true meaning. For example, one of the scriptures we mentioned earlier in the chapter concerning being baptized for the dead would fall into this category. The scripture says, "Otherwise, what will they do who are baptized for the dead, if the dead do not rise at all? Why then are they baptized for the dead?" (1 Corinthians 15:29).

This is one of those more obscure passages. I will not take the time here to delineate the maze of different interpretations given to this verse. However, it perfectly makes the point that many other scriptures shed light on the ordinance of baptism and what it means, and the dead and their spiritual condition. Dr. MacArthur explains, "There have been over 40 suggested explanations for this baptism. As the notes will point out, regardless of how that particular verse is interpreted, the falsehood of dead people having the opportunity to be saved is proven by many other texts that are indisputably clear" (MacArthur 1997, 1727).

The point is well made that other indisputably clear scripture passages shed light on some of the more obscure ones. So, this principle is helpful to avoid going off on a tangent that is completely different from the unity of the Holy Spirit-inspired context of scripture.

These three principles work together under the direction of the Holy Spirit to facilitate "rightly dividing" the Word of Truth. Scripture must be understood within its Holy Spirit-given context and unity. To move away from these principles and the contextual design of the Holy Spirit creates a slippery slope to misuse, misunderstanding, and division.

Experience

There is also the "experience" connection to this sincerity. I am not claiming they have not experienced these things, such as tongues and a prayer language, and they cannot deny what they have actually experienced. I believe they definitely have experienced these things and believe they have received certain spiritual benefits. So for me the question is, are they scripturally accurate or not? Are they actually genuine spiritual gifts that scripture speaks about, or are they some kind of imitation or human-generated experience or in the worst case scenario something that the enemy has counterfeited and is the influence behind?

As you know, experiences can be highly unstable. Certain mountaintop experiences can transport you to Mount Everest emotionally. Other valley experiences can seem to drag us down to the pit. There can be a kind of bipolar range to these events. God has made us creatures that can have a wide range of experiences, and that is good. The events themselves are not the issue. As we will see with some of the pagan religious ceremonies in coming chapters, the real question for us is what is behind these happenings? What is the source behind them, and do they accurately line up with the instruction of scripture?

I believe many of them are simply practicing something they have been told about or taught by others or are continuing an experience they discovered themselves. Either way they sincerely believe that it is from God. Just the other day I was at a place of business and struck up a conversation with a Christian man there. He was sharing with me about the work he does with drug addicts and alcoholics, and I reciprocated with sharing about our mission work in Third World countries with disaster victims and those trapped in unbelievable poverty. It was a sweet time of sharing about our mission work for Christ. I told him I wanted to pray for us as I was about to leave. We joined hands and as I began to pray for God's supernatural blessings on our mission work, he began to speak in some unintelligible sounds with a quick, staccato kind of delivery. I believe this was what he believed was some kind of prayer language to the Lord. I enjoyed my time with him, and as I left we both shared a fond goodbye in the love of Christ.

As we diligently study the scripture, especially in these key passages, I believe we will see that some of these gift experiences do not accurately line up with inspired scripture. This will become much more evident as we do the verse-by-verse study in 1 Corinthians. Because of these scriptural truths, I personally believe that, especially with these wonderful Christian people, these are humanly generated experiences or imitations. Perhaps they have heard about these experiences or perhaps they have watched others practice them, and they have followed in their footsteps. Perhaps they have prayed and asked for an experience and have received it (simply praying for a spiritual experience can be very misleading). This in no way makes them bad people. In fact, I think many of them I know are great people. This is illustrated by so many great characteristics in their lives, not to mention big, giving hearts. With no ill will or negative intention on their part, I believe they practice these experiences sincerely believing they are receiving supernatural benefits. I do believe they are sincere in that belief, but I also firmly believe that their belief scripturally misses the mark.

Buddy, my heart is far from being the legalistic traditionalist that just wants to scripturally crush these errors (there are those out there who seem to lack the heart of Christ in their disagreement). I have tried to force myself to accept some of these things I see in these sweet people. I have wanted to be open in case I missed it somewhere along the line. My heart is for them and I love them. However, even as I have tried to be open to all God wants me to see in this regard, the truth is, once again, confirmed for me. After forty years of walking with the Lord and learning to listen to the Holy Spirit within me, I hear His voice. Once again, through this study of scripture, He is confirming truth I have studied many times through the years. In fact, He is refreshing me and giving me new blessings. So, I have no choice but to stand in the truth He has shown me. That is what I have tried to do through my life, sometimes with a significant cost.

On a personal note, I want to express humble gratitude to those who have had a great impact on my life in the study of God's Word. I am a simple pastor who has been given the privilege of studying under some of the great Bible scholars of our time. These are brilliant men, such as my great friend and mentor Dr. Paige Patterson, along with many other great intellects at Luther Rice Seminary, Criswell College, Dallas Theological Seminary, and pastors of great churches through the years. I could never name them all, as many of them are men I have never met but who have impacted me nonetheless through their spiritually inspired books. The more I study their work, the more I truly know that academically I am "unworthy to loosen their sandal strap." While acknowledging their influence and impact in my life, I must acknowledge the greatest of all influences in my life, which is my precious Holy Spirit Who has been in me and with me all these forty years. He has guided me, directed me, inspired me, lifted me out of the pit of despair, and taught me how to listen to Him. With His guidance, I have tried to be obedient to the Lord's call on my life. So, as a pastor and father, I am simply trying to share His truth in His way with my family and my extended Christian family that God has placed in my life. Please know I have no intention of being offensive to anyone. I am just humbly trying to "rightly divide" the Word of Truth.

Incredible Grace

The grace of God is rich and full, it's wealth beyond compare
It reaches to the lowest hell and finds the sinner there
But how can we describe this grace from God's own heart to ours
A gift so large so full and free it speaks of His great powers

It's deeper than the deepest sea and higher than the stars
It's bigger than our universe, the sun, the moon, and mars
It's greater than the greatest thought the world has ever known
A cross of wood and metal spikes a tomb cut out of stone
It's wider than the greatest width and math cannot conceive
The sum of what was in God's heart when His dear Son did leave

Amazing grace how sweet the sound that saved a wretch like me
I once was lost but now am found, was blind but now I see[1]

It's well beyond my feeble mind the fullness of His grace
But when I see the scars of love, the smile upon His face
Then I will feel the full effect of what He did for me
A grace so great, so high, so deep my raptured soul will see

Then I will fall upon my knees at His amazing grace
And I will feel the softness of His hands upon my face
Then as He gently lifts me up and looks into my eyes
The awesome grace I sang about I'll fully realize.

June 2003

---

[1] "Amazing Grace," written by John Newton, 1779. Public domain.

Part 2: My Study

Chapter 4
The Big Problem

Wickedness

A glaring issue must be exposed in order to have a fuller understanding of the problems concerning the spiritual gifts issue at Corinth. The environment of the city in which the Corinthian believers lived was a problem that affected them greatly. A very big problem within the city itself contributed in direct and indirect ways to the problems in the church. This enormous problem was wickedness, evil, and idolatry. The environment in which they lived was notoriously evil and full of idols. The New Unger's Bible Dictionary states, "The moral pollution of their city, which was notorious, was a continual temptation to them" (Unger 1988, 256).

The city of Corinth in that day was notorious for immorality, especially as it relates to the worship of false gods. Some of these great temples built to honor false gods actually included temple prostitutes. They would actually have sex with temple patrons as part of the ritual of worship.

Dr. Patterson explains, "The ancient Greek city of Corinth was noted more for its licentiousness than for its learning. It was sometimes called the city of Aphrodite. Aristophanes coined the word *korinthiazesthai* to express a reprehensible form of behavior characterized by lust and debauchery. The historian Strabo told of a thousand temple prostitutes inhabiting the Temple of Aphrodite on the Acrocorinth. That the city was the playground for the multifarious groups of sailors and other travelers who entered its gates is indicated by Hegesippius, who called it 'the lounge of Greece,' and by Aristeides, who referred to it as 'a palace of Poseidon'" (Patterson 1983, 12).

This description is also confirmed by The New Unger's Bible Handbook: "Materialism and lust were two vices that plagued the city. Its brisk commercialism fostered the former; the entrenched cult of Aphrodite fostered the latter. The goddess of love (lust) had her temple above the Acrocorinth, served by more than a thousand religious prostitutes. Voluptuous and vicious forms of the goddess worship made Corinth a notorious center of immorality (cf. The Corinthian letters, especially 1 Corinthians 5:1–5). Such terms as 'to corinthianize,' 'Corinthian sickness,' etc., were reminiscent of the moral debauchery of the city" (Unger 1984, 459).

To say that Corinth was a place of immorality and idol worship would be a great understatement. The city was notorious through the ancient world for not only moral filth but also being an epicenter for the perverted worship of false gods. "While this church was zealous and prosperous, it was also prone to great troubles. Corinth was a wealthy commercial city; it was famous even among the heathen for its sensual worship of Venus" (Packer 1995, 596). The Corinthian believers lived in and came out of this incredibly wicked environment.

Their difficulty in breaking away from a terribly corrupt environment in which they had been involved is noted as The New Unger's Bible Handbook states, "It was penned to instruct the recent converts from the lowest and grossest paganism with its vice and sin, so notably practiced at Corinth. . . . It was not easy for these converts to break with their degraded past" (Unger 1984, 489).

These new converts had been involved in some of the grossest sin practiced in Corinth. They had worshiped false gods in degrading ways and had been inoculated by the enemy. Their minds had been continuously corrupted by sexual deviancy, and their bodies had been given over to the practice of wickedness. Over the years of abuse and continuity of evil participation, the darkened practices and what they had been taught was entrenched.

As Paul scolded the Corinthian believers for some of the problems within the church, he said, "Do you not know that the unrighteous will not inherit the kingdom of God? Do not be deceived. Neither fornicators, nor idolaters, nor adulterers, nor homosexuals, nor sodomites, nor thieves, nor covetous, nor drunkards, nor revilers, nor extortioners will inherit the kingdom of God. *And such were some of you.* But you were washed, but you were sanctified, but you were justified in the name of the Lord Jesus and by the Spirit of our God" (1 Corinthians

6:9–11, emphasis added). They had been washed and justified through the blood of Christ and set free by God's grace, but they were not living in that freedom.

The facts of their past wickedness and the continuing evil environment in which they lived and struggled are beyond dispute. This was the "sin city" of its day. It may have been much worse in that they used the sexual deviancy and wickedness in their pagan religious worship. Their worship itself was wickedness.

Having established their past wicked lifestyles and the continuing wicked environment, some of the residual effects seem obvious. Some of the same evil traps they had lived in before were now creeping into the church fellowship. Some of the very issues Paul is dealing with in our discussion are residual carryovers from the lives lived in the past. Though they had been saved through Christ and His atoning blood on the cross, the old, entrenched patterns of living in the flesh were making an ugly return. Not that what Christ had done in them was not sufficient, but that they were not living in the power of who they were in Christ. They were not walking in the Spirit and were, therefore, fulfilling the lusts of the flesh. In a sense, they were forfeiting what Christ had accomplished for them.

These old, entrenched, fleshly patterns seemed to be rearing their ugly heads again. Dr. Patterson enumerates some of these issues. "Although Jesus said that love for one another was the badge of discipleship (John 13:35), nevertheless, they had demonstrated in the following ways the quiescence of that love: (1) the existence of the four divisions in the church (chap.'s 1–4); (2) the toleration of moral decadence within the church (chap. 5); (3) the willingness to go to the civil courts of law in cases against one another (chap. 6) (4) a concern about their own freedom even when it caused others to stumble (chap.'s 8–10); (5) their selfishness at the Lord's table (11:20–21) (6) their selfishness and pride concerning spiritual gifts (chap.'s 12–14)" (Patterson 1983, 230).

Paul gave them a stinging rebuke when he said, "And I, brethren, *could not speak to you as to spiritual people but as to carnal, as to babes in Christ.* I fed you with milk and not with solid food; for until now you were not able to receive it, and *even now you are still not able*; for *you are still carnal.* For where there are envy, strife, and divisions among you, are you not carnal and behaving like mere men" (1 Corinthians 3:1–3, emphasis added).

Ouch! You are still carnal, Paul said. You're still living with the old, fleshly patterns in control. You are like babies I have to feed with the very simplest of spiritual food. You are unable to handle solid spiritual food. You are not progressing. You're not living up to your potential. You have been stunted in your growth and are still living like mere men, instead of spiritually redeemed men who have been set free by the grace of God.

So, seeing this wicked background and environment and seeing its residual effects upon their spiritual lives, the immaturity is undeniable. The church at Corinth is undeniably one of the most spiritually immature churches in the New Testament. Some would argue it is the most spiritually immature church. Whether it is or isn't we don't know, but it would certainly be in the running for the title. For those who had been born again spiritually, it was alarming for Paul to see abuse and deviancy still being practiced.

With these problems in mind, it is no great stretch to see why there were abuses and misuses of the spiritual gifts; they were still living in a selfish, fleshly way. This left an open door for the enemy to cause havoc. He was trying to misuse the gifts and lead these immature believers down the wrong road. He was trying to use abuse, misdirection, imitation, counterfeit, or anything else that would turn these wonderful God-given gifts into tools he could use to mislead.

Ecstatic Utterance

Another religious experience from their past pagan worship was something I believe also crept into their current, carnal worship with the enemy's help. It is sometimes called "ecstatic utterance." Whether we would label it an imitation, counterfeit, or both is not my greatest concern. What is exceedingly clear is that when this ecstatic utterance was practiced within their pagan religious rituals it was not of God. These Corinthians had watched others involved in pagan ecstatic utterance, and many may well have been personally involved. So imagine some of them in their pagan past speaking in ecstatic utterance. It may have occurred in some kind of worked-up frenzy, or it may have been initiated by demonic spirits in this pagan setting, but either way it was used by the enemy to produce bondage, deception, and confusion in people's lives. We know the enemy's modus operandi, "The thief does not come except to *steal, and to kill, and to destroy*" (John 10:10, emphasis added).

These are his reasons. These are his only reasons! He is out to deceive in any way he can. There is nothing he would not use to carry out his reasons. There is nothing he would not use to try to imitate or counterfeit the things of God in order to reach his final goal—leading people away from the truth. And should this really be a great surprise for anyone who has studied God's Word concerning his approach?

In speaking of false apostles who claim to be something they are not, Paul proclaimed, "For such are false apostles, deceitful workers, transforming themselves into apostles of Christ. And no wonder! For *Satan himself transforms himself into an angel of light*. Therefore it is no great thing if *his ministers also transform themselves into ministers of righteousness*, whose end will be according to their works" (2 Corinthians 11:13–15, emphasis added).

Satan usually does not come as some hideous-looking creature with horns, fangs, and blood dripping from his mouth. In most religious settings, it seems he would prefer to appear as an angel of light. That way, he tends to fly under most radars. He will use anything at his disposal to appear one way on the surface but in reality to be deadly underneath.

Many Christians do not even realize that ecstatic utterance was a very real part of some pagan religions. Some Christians today, though sweet and well-intentioned, tend to be in the dark. They are unaware of this history either from lack of study or in some cases an ostrich-like fear. Please be aware, if you're not already, that ecstatic utterance was used by the enemy in pagan religions. If it can be used in any way to mislead, he will use it. If it can be counterfeited and used to subtly misdirect, he will use it. If he can make it appear as something angelic and full of light in the practice of religion, all the better.

In speaking of the ecstatic utterance influence from the Corinthians' previous pagan, religious experiences and the carryover effect into their new lives, Dr. Patterson explains, "These *pneumatika* or *charismata* had come to occupy a place of stupendous importance in the church at Corinth. The mystical, mysterious, and ecstatic nature of the various Greek oracles was still an influence with which to be reckoned in the first century. That the pagan element, having come into the Lord's church in Corinth, would have a tendency toward the reproduction of some of the ecstatic features of their former faith is sad but understandable" (Patterson 1983, 206–207).

This again speaks to the residual effects of their former lives upon their current lives. Having been raised in this pagan environment and repetitiously exposed to and involved in these rituals, they were now struggling to move in a new direction. Their old life patterns were colliding with their new life patterns. Some of the old was creeping in looking like a spiritual lamb when in reality it was the old wolf.

Isn't it interesting that Paul spent a significant amount of time in 1 Corinthians speaking of the relative unimportance of a tongue they were using with no understanding or comprehension as contrasted with prophecy? Concerning their use of a tongue, Paul stated, "Yet in the church I would rather speak five words with my understanding, that I may teach others also, than ten thousand words in a tongue" (1 Corinthians 14:19). Yet in the selfish environment within the church at Corinth, this gift had become extremely prominent. The enemy had used selfishness and a prideful desire for prominence to warp the truth of God's sovereign intention.

Though I will be dealing with this in the exposition of 1 Corinthians chapters 12–14 in later chapters, let me share a few more words about ecstatic utterance. Webster's New Collegiate Dictionary defines ecstatic as, "one that is subject to ecstasies" (Woolf 1981, 357). So I looked above that entry to the word ecstasy and see that the first definition states, "A state of being beyond reason and self-control" (Woolf 1981, 357).

So the definition seems to be, "a person subject to fits of being beyond reason and self-control." It is interesting to note that one of the fruits of the Spirit given in Galatians 5 is "self-control."

Certainly, this visual of someone subject to fits of being beyond reason and self-control would be an accurate picture of someone caught up in a frenzied, pagan religious experience. They would be beyond any human reasoning and self-control. These forces would somehow be channeled through their bodies and senses, making them become a passive instrument.

It seems most everyone agrees that these "ecstatic utterances" would be some kind of unintelligible sounds. Webster's very brief definition of unintelligible is, "not intelligible: obscure" (Woolf 1981, 1270).

So it seems the sounds created for one who is manifesting ecstatic utterances are not intelligible. For most of us, that would fit with the description given above for someone caught up in a frenzied, religious experience.

I realize for some of our sweet friends in the charismatic community who believe in a genuine form of ecstatic utterance, they would claim that though their sounds are unintelligible to others and to the speaker, they are intelligible to God. I suppose in the sense that an omniscient, all-knowing God would know everything, that is certainly true. However, that does pose some other interesting questions.

Judging from scriptural guidelines concerning tongues, we see it is required by God's design that there is an interpreter. If these sounds are unintelligible to everyone except God, how do you interpret unintelligible sounds? I believe the answer would be that a person would be given the supernatural ability to interpret the sounds using the gift of interpretation as mentioned in scripture. That certainly would be the only way this could truly be accomplished genuinely and accurately. This then poses another interesting question.

If these sounds are unintelligible to everyone including the speaker and interpreter, how can you know the interpretation by the interpreter is genuine and accurate? If no one really knows the true meaning of the sounds, how can you be sure that someone who gives an interpretation is delivering what is genuine and accurate? Don't you have to accept by faith that the person giving the interpretation is genuinely gifted and sharing exactly what God has given them—the supernatural ability to interpret directly from Him? Could this possibly leave you open to something that is well-meaning but not really genuine and accurate? Could it be possible this person who has assumed the role of interpreter could be sharing something humanly manufactured or that they have heard before? Could it be that this person assuming the role of interpreter, though a sweet Christian, really does not have the God-given gift of interpretation? Is it possible the enemy would try to intervene and use this for his own purposes? How could you know for sure with something like the inspired Word of God, which is so incredibly important, that you are getting it right? I believe the answer would be that the gift of discernment would be exercised and prevail.

This brings up another interesting question. How could you know for sure that someone who says they have the gift of discernment would get it right? How could you really know they even have the gift of discernment? Could it be they have shared some wisdom that was well-applied in other situations and have decided they do have the gift of discernment? Could it be that a well-meaning brother or sister in Christ who was helped by this person's input in their life exclaimed to them one day, "You have the gift of discernment!"? Once again, don't you have to accept by faith that this person who says they have the gift of discernment truly has it? Don't you have to accept by faith that they are employing this gift exactly as God has led them to and are getting it supernaturally correct? Again, remember, these are unintelligible sounds to everyone within the group. Is it possible the enemy would want to intervene and mislead while everything appears very angelic and light worthy on the surface?

Add to all this someone who has a sense from his or her study of scripture that something is not as it should be. They certainly could not freely accept by faith that these unintelligible sounds are from the Holy Spirit and accurate to God's Word. They also would have difficulty accepting by faith the interpretation of these unintelligible sounds as a message of explanation from God. Additionally, they would also struggle to accept by faith that whoever in the worship service that has the gift of discernment has actually exercised it according to scripture. Let's also consider the provocative thought that this person who has a spiritual red flag going up is a person with the true gift of discernment. Even though they may graciously sit through the service with no response, they would still have in their hearts this same sense of spiritual caution that something is not right.

The response from some concerning those who do not believe the use of these gifts in these ways are scripturally accurate has been varied. Some have said they are immature and not attuned to the Holy Spirit and for this reason do not understand. Others have said they have been taught a theology that blocks them from these wonderful truths. Others have said they have not journeyed deeply into the spiritual truths and are not able to comprehend these things. Still others have said they have not received the baptism of the Holy Spirit, which brings the supernatural ability to exercise and understand these gifts.

We spend our whole life in Christ growing in our walk with Him and gaining maturity. Could it also be possible that a theology, which doesn't believe these uses are accurate to scripture, doesn't block us but actually frees us from the exercises of inaccuracy that also seemed to plague the Corinthian Church? For those who believe we have not journeyed deeply into spiritual truths and are somehow afraid to take the plunge, could it be we have taken a dive into the deep end of the pool and understand more from the Holy Spirit than they think? Concerning those who would claim we have not received the baptism of the Holy

Spirit, which brings the capacity for these things, could it be that we really have been and still do not believe it is scripturally accurate? To take it a step further, could it be that it is actually the Holy Spirit Himself Who is giving the caution? Obviously, with love for those who make these claims, I do believe the latter options are the case and that especially concerning our baptism in the Holy Spirit it has been shown to have happened and to be scripturally accurate.

The questions are many and herein is part of the struggle. How could a God Who would pronounce all the curses of His Word on someone, who would take away or add one word to what He has said, put in place in His church a system of sharing His Word that is so open to misuse, imitation, counterfeit, and corruption, especially knowing Satan as He does? In some of the final words of the biblical Revelation we read, "For I testify to everyone who hears the words of the prophecy of this book: *If anyone adds to these things, God will add to him the plagues* that are written in this book; and *if anyone takes away from the words of the book of this prophecy, God shall take away* his part from the Book of Life, from the holy city, and from the things which are written in this book" (Revelation 22:18–19, emphasis added).

What an incredible statement from God concerning His Word. It is pregnant with the passion of the heart of God. Don't you dare add anything to My Word! Don't you dare take anything away from My Word! Don't you dare change My Word or you will pay an incredibly high price.

Doesn't God demand a clear proclamation of His Word? Even when using the supernatural gift of tongues/languages in Acts chapter 2 at Pentecost, the people from different nations heard a clear proclamation of the "wonderful works of God" in their own language. It was a wonderful authentication of God's power with a clear communication. They heard and they understood!

Even when the supernatural gift of tongues/languages was addressed in the Corinthian Church, didn't the Holy Spirit, through Paul, demand there be an interpreter to give a clear interpretation/proclamation of God's Word or not to use it at all? Didn't He stipulate they should speak only one at a time with an interpreter to make sure everyone heard clearly? Isn't it interesting to see the drastic movement from a clear proclamation of God's Word in an understandable human language at Pentecost with no interpretation needed, all the way to "unintelligible sounds" and "ecstatic utterance" at Corinth with interpretation and discernment needed? There was no mistaking what God was saying at Pentecost, yet there had to be discernment concerning what was real and what was counterfeit at Corinth. There was clarity at Pentecost, yet there was confusion at Corinth.

In summary, it seems clear that their pagan religious experiences from the past and the notoriously wicked environment in which they continued to live contributed to many of the problems Paul addressed in the church. They were certainly very immature, as Paul stated, and very vulnerable to misunderstanding. The bitter divisions, sexual perversion, lawsuits, selfishness at the Lord's Table, and abuse and misuse of spiritual gifts were continuing examples of these residual causes.

He Grew a Cross

The Father saw the seed that fell so very long ago
He knew that seed would be one day a cross where blood would flow
He could have sent a bird to come and take the seed away
Or told His clouds to rain no more till death had come its way

The Father saw the seed that fell so very long ago
He knew that seed would be one day a cross where blood would flow
He could have struck it with disease while young and very small
Or sent a bolt of lightning down to make it burn and fall

The Father saw the seed that fell so very long ago
He knew that seed would be one day a cross where blood would flow
He could have sent a mighty wind to pluck it from the earth
Or sent a builder of a ship to see in it great worth

The Father saw the seed that fell so very long ago
He knew that seed would be one day a cross where blood would flow
He kept it and protected it and nurtured it with rain
An act of love beyond all words He knew the coming pain

He grew a cross, He grew a cross for His beloved Son
He grew a cross while knowing all the hell that was to come
He grew a cross because He knew that I could only be
Saved because His Son was killed for me upon that tree.

March 2008

Chapter 5
The Big Issue

1 Corinthians 12
Unity

The apostle Paul has just finished his scolding corrective in chapter 11 concerning the abuse and misuse of the Lord's Supper. This abuse was so serious due to the fleshly control in their lives that Paul made an astounding statement: due to God's chastisement for this abuse, many of you are weak, many of you are sick, and many of you have died. The problem was so entrenched in their lives, and the spiritual offense was so heinous, that they were experiencing this severe form of God's chastisement. Though God always loves His children, there are times when that love has to be manifested as chastisement. As you continue studying in this book, moving from this deep, spiritual problem into the next deep, spiritual problems in chapter 12, there is an interesting connection issue. In the original writings, there were no chapter and verse designations. Those were added later. So what you have is Paul moving from one serious spiritual problem directly into another serious spiritual problem.

Now in chapter 12, he launches into the next scolding corrective. It is instructive to note in these next three classic chapters of scripture concerning spiritual gifts that they are scolding correctives. The three chapters of scripture used more than any other passages for the study of spiritual gifts are essentially correcting serious errors. These chapters are in some sense, as it pertains to the Corinthians' spiritual abuses, a handbook on how *not* to do it, yet these are the very chapters used by some as an instructive that includes some of their practices.

As we established earlier in this book, the Corinthian Church was riddled with division, selfishness, sexual perversion, and misuse and abuse of a sacred church ordinance and the spiritual gifts. They were arguably the most immature church in the New Testament. As we read this chapter, it becomes clear that this church was not a role model. This was not the church to emulate, especially in their observance of the Lord's Supper and their practice of spiritual gifts. When you study these chapters with these facts in mind, it sheds light on and helps to clarify the problems with which he was dealing.

Paul begins the chapter by telling them he does not want them to be ignorant concerning spiritual gifts. It would seem this is because their misuse and abuse of these gifts was indeed showing ignorance. The division and disunity manifesting itself through the selfish use of these gifts reveals the big issue Paul was addressing. The big issue was "unity" within the Body and in this sad case, the lack thereof. Paul repetitiously states that though there are many different gifts within the Body, it is the same Holy Spirit Who is the source of them all and therefore used rightly would produce divine unity. He speaks of unity again as he says they are all baptized by the Holy Spirit into one body regardless of their background or position in life. He continues to speak of unity as he shows how ludicrous it would be for one part of the physical body to jealously covet being another part of the body. The illustration is extended when one part of the body says to another part of the body, "I don't need you." He ends the chapter by firmly stating that it is God Who has appointed the various gifts within the Church and though some of them may be coveting other's gifts, not everyone has all these gifts.

Many Gifts, the Same Spirit

(Abbreviations BC=Brief Commentary, SN=Study Notes)

12:1, BC—Immediately following the scolding corrective in the last verse of chapter 11 concerning their misuse and abuse of the Lord's Supper, Paul now launches into his corrective on the spiritual gifts. His desire for them concerning spiritual gifts is that they would not be spiritually ignorant of the genuine use of these gifts in a way that is honoring to God and His Word.

SN—It is apparent from this beginning verse that Paul is addressing some very egregious, current problems concerning spiritual gifts in the Corinthian Church. The pagan background many of them had come out of, and were still coming out of, was a corrupting influence upon the gifts and their use within the church. Paul didn't want them to continue in this ignorance and corruption of the spiritual gifts.

12:2, BC—He reminds them of their spiritual bondage in the past. While in this spiritual bondage, they had been controlled and carried away in the practice of idolatry. Their worship and religion revolved around inanimate objects called idols that had no abilities of any kind and, in fact, no life at all. They had been passive passengers led away in this false worship of idols in many different directions with many resulting experiences.

SN—In addressing their pagan past, Paul speaks of them as being "carried away" to these dumb idols. No doubt those pagan religious rituals with frenzied and bizarre actions are in view. Whether it was involuntary fits of the body jerking in various directions under the influence of evil spirits or whether it was being caught up in mystical bouts of ecstatic utterance we don't know. Whatever the case was, they had been controlled and "carried away" in their evil practice of worshiping dumb idols. Vine defines *dumb*, "*aphonos*, lit., voiceless" (Vine 1966, 343).

These dumb idols—literally without a voice—controlled the people involved with them. Obviously, this was because the enemy was the source behind them. Now think of someone in the city of Corinth with this entrenched background being immediately swept into the church after placing his or her faith in Christ. The possibility of severe spiritual problems becomes obvious.

12:3, BC—On the basis of this evil and false belief system to which they had been in bondage and had experienced many things, Paul wanted them to know a couple of absolutes. First, no one who is being controlled by the Holy Spirit of God will ever call Jesus cursed. Second, the only way someone can truly confess that Jesus is Lord is to be controlled by the Holy Spirit of God.

SN—Because of this pagan background and the many false prophets involved in it and possibly even some in the church, Paul gives this spiritual test. It reveals the fingerprint of the enemy when someone is calling Jesus accursed. The Holy Spirit of God will never lead someone to make this confession. The second part of the test is that no one can truly confess Jesus is Lord unless they are being controlled by the Holy Spirit of God. This test could be clearly applied to false teachers and false prophets who were slandering Christ in the common language of the people. The question might be asked, would this test be harder to apply to someone who was speaking in ecstatic utterance, and could that be a scheme of the enemy to enter through the back door?

12:4, BC—Because of the factions and divisions within their fellowship, Paul wants to make a clear point. Though there are many different kinds of genuine spiritual gifts within the church, he wanted them to understand that they all have the same Holy Spirit of God as their source.

SN—Due to the jealousies and coveting of certain spiritual gifts within the church, Paul is trying to draw their attention to their common source. Though there are many different kinds of genuine spiritual gifts at work within the church, it is the same Holy Spirit Who is the source behind them. The only way for these various spiritual gifts to function according to God's plan is to recognize the Holy Spirit as the source and to function under His control.

12:5, BC—Building on the truth in verse 4, he says though there are many different kinds of ministries within the church, they all have the same Lord as their source.

SN—This original language word for *ministries* or *administrations* is one that has to do with serving or service. It is the root word from which we get our word *deacon* and has to do with serving others and meeting their needs within the Body of Christ.

12:6, BC—Building further upon this truth, he says there are many different kinds of activities within the church, but they all have the same God as their source. It is God Who works in and through all these activities to accomplish His sovereign purposes.

SN—The call to unity with God as the unifying source couldn't be any clearer. The disunity evident in the Corinthians' selfish exercise of spiritual gifts, ministries, and activities was devastating to the fellowship and revealed a dysfunctional testimony. Paul was calling them away from divisiveness and back to the supernatural unity of God's design.

12:7, BC—Paul explains to them that the manifestations of these spiritual gifts are given by God for a specific purpose. God sovereignly chooses to give gifts to each one within the Body of Christ in order to benefit all. It is not God's intention for them to be used for the selfish, personal benefit of an individual but to be used in such a way that it profits the whole Body of Christ.

SN—The main point of this verse is an important one for the Corinthians to hear. In spite of all the division, jealousy, and selfishness going on within the Church, they need to clearly understand the reason God has given these grace gifts. These gifts are given to each one specifically for the profit or benefit of the whole Body.

Also, it is interesting to note that Paul says they are given to "each one." Though some may have felt they did not have a gift and were not as valuable to the Body, we see here that each one has been given a gift or gifts to use in order to benefit the whole Body.

12:8, BC—Now, Paul begins to enumerate some of these spiritual gifts with this same thought in mind. To one person within the Body of Christ, God gives the word of wisdom through the Holy Spirit. To another person, God gives the word of knowledge through the same Holy Spirit. It is interesting to note the repetition of the word *same* within these few verses. The same Spirit in verse 4. The same Lord in verse 5. The same God in verse 6. The same Spirit in verses 8, 9 and 11. They needed to understand it was the same God giving these grace gifts to each of them individually for the same purpose and that was for the benefit of the whole Body.

SN—The word of knowledge is a gift in which God gives a person supernatural insight and understanding in a specific situation. The word of wisdom is a gift in which God gives the supernatural ability to apply the insight and understanding according to God's design and plan. Dr. Patterson explains the distinction between them. "The distinction between the two seems to be that the 'word of knowledge' refers to a supernatural comprehension of the facts of a particular situation, whereas 'word of wisdom' refers to the supernatural endowment of being able to take what is revealed in the word of knowledge and apply it correctly to the circumstances and situations of life in a pragmatic way" (Patterson 1983, 211).

It seems clear Paul is exercising both gifts within this passage. He is exercising supernatural insight and understanding concerning the gifts as they are being used in Corinth. He is also exercising the supernatural ability to apply this supernatural insight and understanding according to God's design and plan. His application is to correct the abuse and misuse of the spiritual gifts and to give accurate guidance.

With the wide-ranging proclamations and claims concerning these gifts, it is important to note that when God genuinely gives a gift it will never be in contradiction to His Word.

12:9, BC—Paul continues with the same repetition by saying that God gives to another person within the Body of Christ the gift of faith by the same Holy Spirit. To another person, God gives the gifts of healings by the same Holy Spirit.

SN—In this verse, Paul speaks of two more spiritual grace gifts. The gift of faith is a supernatural ability beyond the faith to trust Christ in salvation. This is a gift that when in operation makes very little sense to the world. Dr. Lowery explains, "Faith as a spiritual gift is probably an unusual measure of trust in God beyond that exercised by most Christians" (Walvoord and Zuck 1983, 533).

This would be the supernatural ability to trust God and move forward in the face of difficulty, distress, danger, etc. This gift sees a way where there seems to be no way. This gift sees God's power and sufficiency to face, and even run toward, the giants. This gift looks at the Red Sea and sees a dry path.

To another is given the gifts of healings. It is interesting to note the plurality designated here as "gifts of healings." This may refer to the situational giving of this gift in many different circumstances as God sovereignly chooses. Paul himself having this gift would be a prime illustration of the situational nature of the gifts of healings. Dr. Patterson speaks to this issue concerning Paul when he writes, "For example, he healed the father of Publius on the island of Melita (Acts 28:8), but he left Trophimus sick in Miletus (2 Tim. 4:20). In 1 Timothy 5:23 he advised medicinal treatment for Timothy's chronic gastrointestinal problem rather than simply healing him. In Philippians 2:25–27, he felt the helplessness of being unable to do anything about Epaphroditus, who was ill to the point of death but then graciously spared by God. Furthermore, in the case of his own circumstance, his 'thorn in the flesh' remained despite three appeals for its removal (2 Cor. 12:7–10). The fact that it was specifically related to the flesh strongly argues for the possibility of some physical malady" (Patterson 1983, 213).

It seems this was a supernatural ability given by God to heal sicknesses and restore health according to His sovereign plan and purpose. This purpose certainly included authenticating His powerful work to others through these leaders of the infant Church.

12:10, BC—He continues the list of spiritual gifts given to individuals within the Body of Christ. To one person, God gives the gift of working miracles, to another the gift of prophecy, to another discerning of spirits, to another different kinds of tongues and to another the interpretation of tongues.

SN—The gift of working miracles is a supernatural ability to do things that are humanly impossible.

Numerous miracles are observed in scripture in the lives of the apostles and other disciples who followed Christ. Again, we must remember this was not a gift of power just to show power within the life of an individual. God was authenticating that what these leaders were saying about Christ was true and that it was His power behind it so that it was undeniable. Dr. W. A. Criswell gives a wonderful explanation when he explains, "What, then, is the purpose of the miraculous? Miracles are for introduction, for authentication, for corroboration, for substantiation. There have been times in the economy of God when they were mightily needed to introduce a new life, a new dispensation. They bore a special testimony at the beginning of each new age. The creation story (Genesis 1–3) is filled with miracles. The introduction of the law through Moses is filled with miracles. The revival under Elijah and Elisha, in the dark days of apostasy when it seemed that worship of the true God would die from the earth, is filled with miracles. The introduction of the Christian era, under Jesus and the apostles, is filled with miracles. The consummation of the age recounted in the Apocalypse is filled with miracles" (Criswell 1966, 148). God always has a design and purpose for what He does, including the gift of miracles.

Another supernatural grace gift from God was prophecy. This gift seems to include two main elements. One element was the supernatural ability to foretell events before they happened. As many prophets did in scripture, they would predict future events by the supernatural power of their omniscient God Who knows all and is outside of time. The other element was the supernatural ability to forth-tell or proclaim the truths of God's Word with God's power in a way that impacted lives and was beyond the mere communication of words.

Dr. A. T. Robertson says this was, "Not always prediction, but a speaking forth of God's message under the guidance of the Holy Spirit" (Robertson 1931, 169).

Dr. Patterson comments after an explanation of the original word, "The New Testament gift of prophecy, then, has two phases associated with it: a gift to know future events and the gift of public proclamation of the Word of God" (Patterson 1983, 215).

Remember that during the beginning years of the new Church, they did not have the completed scriptures of the New Testament. God was communicating His Word supernaturally through these leaders. Dr. MacArthur explains, "In the early church, before the New Testament was complete, certain prophets were used by God on occasion to exhort the church with messages inspired as the prophet spoke. That was necessary to instruct the churches in matters that were not yet covered by Scripture. This revelatory aspect of prophecy was unique to the apostolic era" (MacArthur 1992, 69). They were gifted by God to speak the truths of God's Word and also the future events of God's Word before it was written and recorded. This was before the time when the New Testament scripture was completed and the fearful warning was given in Revelation 22:18–19 to not add to or take anything away from the words of the book of this prophecy. Now that God's Word is written, recorded, and completed, and He has warned us fearfully not to add to or take away from His Word, we dare not call our additional words that are spoken today, words of prophecy from God on an equal footing with those canonized in scripture. Our ministry today is to forth-tell or proclaim the already revealed Word of God in the power of the Holy Spirit.

Another spiritual grace gift given by God was the discerning of spirits. This word *discern* means to be able to ascertain, detect, determine, differentiate, and distinguish what is genuine and what is not. Dr. A. T. Robertson says this was, "A most needed gift to tell whether the gifts were really of the Holy Spirit and supernatural (cf. so-called 'gifts' today) or merely strange though natural or even diabolical (1 Tim. 4:1, 1 John 4:1 f.)" (Robertson 1931, 169–170).

It is important to remember the enemy is always trying to infiltrate the kingdom work of God. There were false prophets in the Old Testament; there were false prophets in the New Testament and most definitely false prophets in the extremely pagan environment at Corinth. It was, and is, critically important to know whether a message or so-called gift is genuinely given by God or is not.

Another of these grace gifts given by God was different kinds of tongues. Please note the word *different* in the New King James Version is in italics, which simply means it was not part of the original language and added by the translators. This word *different* has caused some of the confusion of our day when used as a proof text of sorts to refer to ecstatic utterance. Without the word *different*, though it is implied in one sense, we simply have "kinds of tongues" and must ascertain within the context of scripture its true meaning.

Let's first consult the writings of an authority. Dr. Spiros Zodhiates is a Greek who was born on the island of Cyprus and raised by Greek parents. After completing his Greek education, he also studied at American University in Cairo, Egypt, and New York University in the United States. He holds several degrees, is a recognized authority on the Greek New Testament, and served as editor of an edition of the Modern Greek New Testament. Dr. Zodhiates explains, "What does 'divers kinds of tongues' mean? The same expression is used in verse 28, where it is rendered 'diversities of tongues,' and is again mentioned as one of the gifts bestowed on members of the body of Christ. The expression in Greek is *genee gloossoon*. The word *genos* in this instance means 'class, kind, species, families.' It is the same word from which the English word 'genealogies' is derived, meaning the history of families. This would make *genee gloossoon* mean 'kinds, classes, or families of languages,' and since incomprehensible ecstatic utterances could hardly be classified, it must refer to known human languages" (Zodhiates 1983, 60).

Dr. Patterson also confirms the genuine meaning as used in this instance as he writes, "'Tongue' (*glossa*) demonstrably means the ability to speak various known languages which had not been studied by the one possessing this gift. The purpose of the speaking was twofold: (a) the proclamation of the good news of salvation in Christ to those who otherwise could not have understood and (b) the authentication of the Gospel messenger and his message. Two lines of argument establish this as the genuine intent of the apostle and the real meaning of the gift.

"First, in [1 Cor.] 14:21 Paul argued that the law contained the prophecy that God would speak to His people with 'other tongues and other lips.' This quotation of Isaiah 28:11 most certainly refers to the use of actual existing languages. The second line of argumentation derives from the first instance of the use of the gift of tongues, namely, the day of Pentecost which is recorded in Acts 2. In that passage when the miracle occurred, the people coming together '. . . were confounded, because that every man heard them speak in his own language' (Acts 2: 6). They further expressed their amazement by saying, 'and how hear we every man in our own tongue, wherein we were born?' (Acts 2:8). And again, 'we do hear them speak in our tongues [*glossa*, the same word] the wonderful works of God' (Acts 2:11). That the gift of tongues is then a reference to the use of a language, not heretofore studied, for the purpose of communicating the gospel and authenticating the gospel messenger seems irrefutable. The question remaining as to whether or not a second gift of tongues was present at Corinth will be answered in chapter 14" (Patterson 1983, 215–216).

What is beyond legitimate debate is that the genuine use of the gift of tongues as clearly given by the Holy Spirit of God at Pentecost was the gift of speaking another, known human language without having previously studied the language. It was clearly communicated in their language, clearly understood by them in their language and clearly astonished them. They heard the wonderful works of God clearly with no confusion exactly as God intended. The misuse and abuse of this spiritual gift as it was being used at Corinth will be addressed in the commentary on chapter 14.

The final spiritual grace gift in this list is the interpretation of tongues. This was a supernatural ability given by God to interpret a language that the group or even the interpreter did not understand. In order for there to be any benefit to the Body, which we have seen is God's purpose in giving these gifts and any genuine authentication of God's involvement, there would need to be a clear proclamation and communication of God's words. Without this clear interpretation, there was to be no use of this gift. One of the obvious reasons for this stipulation was the Corinthians in their selfishness and pride were self-promoting. Their motives had been warped and they were trying to exhibit power. It is obvious God was not pleased and this was absolutely not His intention. "God resists the proud, But gives grace to the humble" (1 Peter 5:5).

12:11, BC—With all of these spiritual gifts just mentioned, Paul once again hones in on his main point, which is that the same Holy Spirit works in and through all of these gifts. This same Holy Spirit sovereignly distributes these gifts to individuals within the Body of Christ according to His perfect will, which has a divine, unified purpose.

SN—It is obvious at this point that the repetition of the word *same* is Paul's equivalent of making a statement and then placing three exclamation points at the end. It is the same Holy Spirit Who has given all these gifts to individuals within the Body and works in and through all of them to accomplish His sovereign purpose and plan. He distributes them according to His divine will. The way the Corinthians were misusing and abusing the spiritual gifts for their own selfish motives and purposes clearly reveals their disjointed experiences were not being directed and controlled by this same Holy Spirit.

Many Gifts, Unity

12:12, BC—He continues to address the terrible disunity within the church with an explanation concerning unity. Even as we realize that the body is one body with many different parts, we must also remember that all the members of that one body, even though there are many of them, are still one body. It is the same way in the Body of Christ.

SN—Of course, the illustration is being used as a word picture to speak of the unified Body of Christ. This is clearly a description of the way the Body of Christ is to function according to the divine design of God.

12:13, BC—In one of the clearest statements on spiritual unity in the Body of Christ, Paul states that by the same Holy Spirit, we were all baptized into this one Body of Christ. It now makes no difference whether you are Jewish or Greek. It now makes no difference whether you are a slave or whether you are a free person. Your race and position in life now have no bearing on this new unity. Now everyone in this Body of Christ has been made to partake of and be indwelled by the same Holy Spirit.

SN—Continuing the statement of unity in verse 12, Paul now addresses one of the most crucial of all the unifying experiences. Everyone within the Body of Christ has been baptized by the same Holy Spirit. The former walls and barriers have been completely broken down through this unified experience. The former separation between Jews and Gentiles is erased spiritually through this unified baptism. The social strata of society between the haves and have-nots is demolished spiritually through this unified baptism. All have been unified together through this partaking of the same Holy Spirit.

12:14, BC—Paul says, and the fact of the matter is, this Body of Christ is not just one member but is made up of many different members working in unity. One member of the Body acting independently is a false representation of the Body of Christ.

SN—The Body of Christ is not one kind of member from one race or one social background. It is made up of many different kinds of members from all races and backgrounds that work in unity together.

12:15, BC—Now Paul uses some ludicrous illustrations to make his point concerning the disunity within the Corinthian Church. It also reveals the jealousy and selfishness of some who were coveting the spiritual gifts of others. If a foot decided to say, "Because I am not a hand, I am not part of the body," does that make it so? Isn't the foot still part of the body?

SN—Paul again is addressing some of the petty and immature quarrels among those with various spiritual gifts. If the foot wanted to be a hand but could not be and made a claim that it was not part of the body at all, does that really mean it is a fully independent functioning part on its own? This was an illustration that described some of the jealousy and coveting going on with those in the Corinthian Church who wanted a gift other than their own. The hand is, of course, much more visible than the foot, which may refer to some of them coveting the higher profile and more visible gifts.

12:16, BC—With the same kind of illustration, Paul continues. If an ear decided to say, "Because I am not an eye, I am not part of the body," does that make it so? Isn't the ear still part of the body?

SN—Again, he speaks to the same issue as in verse 15 with the ear and the eye. The eyes are one of the first and most colorful parts of the body that people see. They give sight; they show expression and emotion and can move quickly and freely. Perhaps being upfront, colorful, and emotional was a much more appealing gift to some who were more functional in roles behind the scenes.

12:17, BC—Now he takes the illustration a step further to show the result of the disunity. If the whole body were actually only an eye with its gift of sight, where would the needed gift of hearing be? If the whole body were actually only an ear with its gift of hearing, where would the needed gift of smelling be?

SN—To show the inability to truly function within God's plan and purpose as the Body of Christ with this jealous attitude, he illustrates with a ridiculous word picture. What if the whole Body of Christ were made up of only one particular, high-profile gift, such as an eye? Where would the other critical needed gifts be, such as hearing? Or if the whole Body of Christ were made up of only the one functional support gift, such as hearing, where would the important gift of smelling be? The meaning is obvious. He wants them to see that the Body of Christ cannot function according to God's design with one gift. God designed them all to work in unity with each other to be a fully functioning body.

12:18, BC—Paul now explains what they need to understand concerning the different gifts. It is God Who has sovereignly placed each one of the members in the Body according to His sovereign will. It is not for the members of the Body to decide what they will be or what they will not be. It is God's design according to His sovereign choice.

SN—God is the One Who has set the members in place within the Body of Christ with their designated gifts. God's special care for each of them as individuals is seen in the phrase, "each one of them." There are no unimportant or unneeded individuals. God has given each of them a gift that is important to the whole. All these gifts have been given not based on what others might want but just as it pleased the Lord.

12:19, BC—Paul asks the question, "If all of these parts of the body were one kind of member, where would the whole body be?" How ludicrous would it be to have a grouping of big feet, big hands, big ears, big eyes, or big noses acting as if they were a whole body?

SN—If all of the members of the Body had the same spiritual gift, where would the functioning Body with all its other gifts and abilities be? Though many of them may have been coveting one of the same, exciting, high-profile gifts, the Body would be crippled and deformed without all of the other functioning spiritual gifts.

Years ago when we lived in Dallas, Texas, I was at Baylor Hospital. My wife was having surgery that day and after we said goodbye, they took her down the hall and through the surgical area doors. Knowing I would have a couple hours until she would be in recovery, I went walking. I walked all over the building just observing and killing time. As I walked through the lobby, an incredible sight caught my eye. It was a little shocking, and I have never again seen anything like it. Behind glass in an exhibit were rows and rows of hands. I was intrigued by it and began to look closely. There were four walls of display cases that were filled with exact casts of famous people's hands. Hands of famous doctors, musicians, athletes, artists, presidents, actors, astronauts, business legends, conductors, actresses, and on and on. I found it captivating. Some were big, some small, some short, some long, some young, some old, but all were unique. Some hands that caught my attention in particular were: Van Cliburn, a pianist with long, nimble, skilled fingers; Dr. Christian Barnard, heart surgeon with fairly large, strong-looking fingers; Andres Segovia, guitarist with large fingers and hands for such skill on guitar strings; Roger Staubach, NFL quarterback with injured, crooked fingers, which had been broken many times; Meadowlark Lemon, basketball star with incredibly long fingers; Peggy Fleming, ice skater with beautiful and elegant fingers; and basketball legend Wilt Chamberlain's hands were displayed immediately next to Willie Shoemaker, a great jockey. The contrast of Wilt's incredibly large hands next to Willie's incredibly small hands looked almost unreal. There was also Greer Garson, a famous actress with very wrinkled, elderly hands. David Copperfield, the famous magician, had very smooth, nimble-looking hands. Andre the Giant, a professional wrestler, had hands so crazy large that you have to see it to believe it.

All of those incredible hands that had saved lives, moved hearts with music, inspired crowds with athletic endurance, painted masterpieces, ruled countries, brought movies to life, traveled into space, led huge companies to success, conducted great orchestras, and portrayed great characters had one thing in common. Those skilled hands that had achieved the highest levels of success were connected to a functioning body. In most, if not all of these lives, the whole body had to be functioning at a very high level of unity to achieve their amazing success. If they were amputated, by themselves they would have no way of accomplishing these great feats of skill and inspiration.

This is Paul's point. Without connection and unity, the individual parts cannot function according to God's design. All of the great potential of each part is forfeited when it is disconnected and self-centered. It loses the body dynamic, which God designed.

12:20, BC—So Paul stresses the point again, as he wants them to understand this genuine scriptural concept of the Body. Yes, absolutely there are many different members in the Body with different gifts, but all of them together still make up only one body.

SN—In this verse and the verses surrounding it, Paul is demanding that they see and understand their vital connection. Due to the misuse of their diversity, they had eroded their unity. What God had designed as a unified Body had now become like the displaced pieces of a puzzle strewn all over a table.

12:21, BC—Within this one body, the eye cannot stand alone and say to the hand, "I don't need you." Neither can the head stand alone and say to the feet, "I don't need you." These statements would be ludicrous because these body parts *do* need each other to function as the whole body should.

SN—The divisions within the Corinthian Church had become so pronounced they were actually severing ties with one another. One person was trying to use his spiritual gift independently without the function of the other spiritual gifts. These divisions and jealousies were causing the Body of Christ to become deformed and nonfunctioning.

12:22, BC—There is no way this would work. In fact, Paul wanted them to understand that in reality, those members of the Body who seem to be weaker individually are actually very necessary. Though some parts have a higher profile and seem to be stronger than others, the parts that have a lower profile and may seem to be weaker than others are still very necessary to the Body.

SN—Paul says no, this is absolutely wrong. God has divinely placed individuals with lower-profile, *seemingly* weaker gifts within the Body of Christ as critically important parts that enable the whole Body to function properly according to His will. In the churches I have pastored over the years, there have always been an army of people serving behind the scenes. I was the one seen most often, but they were the ones with the lower-profile gifts that really got the work done. While serving, giving, helping, and preparing they would use their gifts to serve the Lord in ways no one else would ever see. Without them, the Body could not function.

12:23, BC—Those parts of the Body that we might think are recognized less are actually parts we give greater honor and recognition to. Also, there are parts of the Body that are not seen openly and tend to be hidden from view.

SN—With the proper humility and unity that should be manifested within the Body of Christ, we lift up and honor those who have been given gifts that have a lower profile, such as the gift of helps and service gifts. Praise the Lord for the faithful servants who stand in a room and sort clothes or bag food for those in need. I also think of the people who come early when nobody is there to turn the lights on, open the doors, and prepare the facilities for people to worship. In addition, individuals with gifts not intended to function openly (unpresentable parts) are more modest and discrete as they exercise their spiritual gifts in order to benefit the whole Body. No one ever sees the hard work of the person cleaning the church through the week, but they certainly see it (and usually comment on it) if that hidden, service work is not done. I think of my friend Ken who has gone faithfully to the nursing homes every Sunday for over thirty years to love on and minister to our precious people who are not even able to leave their beds. No one ever sees that wonderful ministry and sacrifice.

12:24, BC—The parts of our bodies that are usually seen openly have no need of a lower profile or to be hidden from view. Remember, it is our sovereign God Who designed the Body, and it was by His intentional purpose to give greater honor and recognition to lower-profile gifts.

SN—The list of these lower profile, helping, and service gifts is unlimited. I think of my brother Fred who cares for my parents round the clock in a little house that almost never has visitors. My mom and dad have been faithfully serving the Lord in ministry for fifty-five years in churches all over the country and in missions all over the world. Now because of their failing health they are unable to even go to church. Though his ministry is unseen by most people, it is evident to God. I also think of my friend Keith who ministers to people at a rescue mission in a little town. When I was there one night, one of the homeless people got sick in the bathroom and vomited. Keith was the first one of us to volunteer to go in and clean up the vomit, and he grabbed some cleaning supplies with a joyful attitude and a smile on his face. His ministry is rarely seen by people but evident to our Father. God has given an extra measure of honor to those individuals with spiritual gifts that are not as flashy and high profile as others, so that the Body of Christ will not degenerate into the haves and have-nots. Keep God's design; it will work fine!

12:25, BC—The very reason God designed the Body this way was so there would be no internal division (breakup, alienation, discord, dissension, disunion, faction, fracture, rupture, falling out, severance, rift, split). God's purpose was that each of the parts of the body should have the same kind of loving care for each other.

SN—God's design of the gifts properly functioning together will manifest loving unity. With the flesh in control, as it was in the Corinthian Church, the functioning of the gifts actually manifested bitter division. God's design was that the individual members within the Body of Christ would all have the same loving care and compassion for each other, exhibiting the sacrificial love of Christ.

Paul addressed this when he wrote to the Philippians and said, "Fulfill my joy by being like-minded, having the same love, being of one accord, of one mind. Let nothing be done through selfish ambition or conceit, but in lowliness of mind let each esteem others better than himself. Let each of you look out not only for his own interests, but also for the interests of others" (Philippians 2:2–4).

12:26, BC—God's design of the Body is revealed when one single part is suffering and all the other members are suffering along with it. Or in another way, if one single part of the Body is being honored and recognized, all the other members are rejoicing with that one member.

SN—The true unity within the Body of Christ is most clearly seen when one individual member is suffering and all of the rest of the Body is compassionately suffering with him. They all share one another's burdens. This true unity is also seen when one member is honored and recognized and all of the rest of the Body is rejoicing in that honor and recognition. They share the burdens together, and they rejoice in the honor together. This was what the Corinthians especially needed and was a rebuke to their division and selfishness. They were not living in the freedom and grace that Christ had given them.

Many Gifts, God Appointed

12:27, BC—Now here is what I want you to see very clearly. You are the Body of Christ and each of you are the individual members of that Body.

SN—Because you have placed your faith in Jesus Christ, you are actually part of the Body of Christ. Each of you are gifted members that make up that Body. Though you were pagans before, now you are changed inside through salvation in Christ and have the Holy Spirit of God living in you. You're the Body of Christ and you need to live according to God's design.

12:28, BC—Within the Body of Christ, God has appointed these specific parts of that Body. First, He has appointed apostles; second, prophets; third, teachers; after these He has appointed those whom He gifts to do His miracles, then those whom He gifts to use His supernatural healing, then those He gifts with helping, then those He gifts with administrating, then those He gifts with different kinds of tongues.

SN—Paul now enumerates some of those gifts. The first three are apostles, prophets, and teachers. Dr. Paige Patterson delineates these first three when he writes, "The first three offices indicated and specifically ordered suggest that these offices belong, at least primarily, to the pastoral leadership of the church. There is no question that the first, the gift of the apostle, ceased with the end of the apostolic era and the death of those thus appointed. As for the prophets, we have already seen that at least one of the functions of the prophet, that of delineating the future through special revelation, also evidently ceased with the coming of the written New Testament. However, the element of prophecy that encompasses public proclamation is still among the spiritual gifts. Certainly the third category of teacher, which may correspond to the pastor and teacher category of Ephesians 4:11, is a gift that continues in the church" (Patterson 1983, 225).

The next gift in this list is the gift of miracles. This gift was discussed in verse 10 of this chapter.

The next gift in this list is the gifts of healings. This gift was discussed in verse 9 of this chapter.

The next gift in this list is the gift of helps. This is one of my favorite gifts because it truly manifests the heart of Christ in its compassionate help to others. Vine states, "It is mentioned in 1 Corinthians 12:28, as one of the ministrations in the local church, by way of rendering assistance, perhaps especially of help ministered to the weak and needy" (Vine 1966, 213). Though this is not one of the high-profile gifts, it is certainly one that is at the core of the true love Paul teaches on in the following chapter. This gift speaks of true love and motives that are selfless. Though most of the working of this gift is seen by very few, there is no clearer picture of Christ. This gift is a picture of James 1:27 which says, "Pure and undefiled religion before God and the Father is this: *to visit orphans and widows in their trouble,* and to keep oneself unspotted from the world" (James 1:27, emphasis added). This gift sees someone with a burden and actually gets under the burden to lift it off of them.

The next gift in this list is the gift of administrations. This word is also translated as "governments" in some versions. Dr. Patterson gives us a clear description as he writes, "The gift of 'governments,' therefore, has nothing whatsoever to do with ruling or with any legislative function but should be translated 'counsel.' While those with the gift of 'helps' were helping predominantly with the physical burdens of the people, those with the gifts of 'governments' were apparently sharing advice and counsel in critical spiritual and emotional matters" (Patterson 1983, 226).

The next gift in this list is the gift of varieties of tongues. This gift was already discussed in verse 10 of this chapter.

12:29, BC—Having just explained to them these different giftings to different individual parts within the Body, he now asks several questions to make a point that not all the individual parts of the Body have the same gifting. The obvious answer to these questions is no. He asks, Are all of the individual parts of the body apostles? Are all prophets? Are all teachers? Are all workers of miracles?

SN—After spending significant time in this chapter explaining that God gives different gifts to different individuals within the Body of Christ for the good of the whole Body, now Paul stresses the point once again. Some of the Corinthians were coveting gifts they did not have because of the nature of those gifts. Presumably, some of them were even attempting to exercise gifts they had not been given by God's divine choice. In a sense, they were trying to imitate or mimic those particular gifts. In order to once again stress the point that not all the members of the Body of Christ have the same gifts, Paul begins to ask these rhetorical questions. Are all apostles? Are all prophets? Are all teachers? Are all workers of miracles? They would have understood clearly that not all of them possessed these specific, spiritual grace gifts, and the answer was an obvious no.

12:30, BC—He continues this barrage of questions to make his point. Do all of the individual parts of the Body have God's gifts of healings? Do all have the gift to speak with various tongues? Do all have the gift of interpreting? The point is crystal clear. Though there are many different members of the Body, they do not all have the same gifting from God. God has given them different gifts according to His sovereign purpose.

SN—These rhetorical questions continue as he hammers home the point. Perhaps there were those in the Corinthian Church who believed they did possess all the spiritual gifts or possibly that all the members possessed all the spiritual gifts. Perhaps they believed they possessed all the spiritual gifts even if some were more pronounced and some were more latent or as yet undeveloped. Perhaps some believed they just had to grow into the use of them as they learned and progressed to higher levels of spirituality. This would, of course, have led to all kinds of pride and jealousy problems between the haves and have-nots and between the spiritually enlightened and the spiritually unenlightened. Paul makes the point very clear through these questions with the expected negative answer that not all of them had the same spiritual gifts. God had given them different gifts so that all the different gifts working together in love and harmony would produce a vibrant, strong, unstoppable Body of Christ.

12:31, BC—Paul says, "My spiritual direction to you is for your strong desire to be channeled toward the best gifts that God has for you. But with all this in mind, I want to show you a more exceptional, superb way to function and to use those gifts within the Body."

SN—It is obvious from the whole import and theme of this chapter that he is not telling them to selfishly covet the most flashy and prominent gifts, such as the gift of tongues, in order to be self-promoting and prideful. He is not telling them to covet a spiritual gift that God has not divinely assigned to them because they are not happy with the gift God has given them. In fact, that is exactly what some of them have been doing with destructive results. He has been correcting those errors, and he made it very clear that God has assigned the gifts to individuals according to His perfect plan and design for the Body as a whole. It seems Paul is saying, "It is fine for you to have a strong, godly desire to exercise the best and most useful gifts to build up and benefit the whole Body of Christ, and I encourage you in that; however, even with that in mind, I want to show you the most excellent way to function according to God's plan and purpose." Dr. A. T. Robertson said, "I show you a supremely excellent way. Chapter 13 is this way, the way of love already laid down in 8:1 concerning the question of meats offered to idols (cf. 1 John 4:7)" (Robertson 1931, 175).

With all of the furor over the exercise of spiritual gifts and the resulting problems in the Corinthian Church, Paul now wants to share the highest priority of all. The priority of love.

He Chose the Cross

He didn't call His angels to strike the mob that day
Twelve legions would have answered and swept them all away
His love looked past the anger to souls who had a debt
His love looked all the way to me, my awful price He met

He didn't slay the soldiers, each lash upon His back
One word from God incarnate would stop them in their tracks
Behind the whips and curses He saw the souls in need
He chose to let them swing their whips and do their awful deed

He didn't come down early to leave the pain and loss
To stop the mouths of those who mocked and put them on the cross
He let them speak because He knew the darkness they were in
The darkness that would be destroyed the victory He would win

He didn't stop the judgment, each moment like an hour
He hung till it was finished to show His love and power
Each time you think of Jesus and what He did for you
May you then be reminded of all He did not do

He chose the cross, He felt the pain, He shed His blood for you
His love was on display that day in what He didn't do
He didn't call, He didn't slay, He didn't leave the tree
He didn't stop the judgment, to show His love for me.

March 2008

Chapter 6
The Big Priority

1 Corinthians 13
Love

Now Paul moves into the next scolding corrective in chapter 13. After revealing the fragmented, dysfunctional Body in chapter 12 with its resulting disunity, he now moves on to the highest priority of all: godly love.

With all of the rush to exercise the spiritual grace gifts within the Church, the Corinthians had rushed past the highest priority of all. That highest priority of all was the commandment from Jesus Himself when He said, "A new commandment I give to you, that you love one another; as I have loved you, that you also love one another. By this all will know that you are My disciples, if you have love for one another" (John 13:34–35).

This was not a suggestion from Jesus. This was a commandment to the apostles from the Savior Himself. It was a commandment with a very high standard. The standard was to love one another as Jesus loved us. The commandment was to truly love each other within the Body of Christ with a godly, sacrificial kind of selfless love. When this kind of godly, sacrificial love is being exercised within the Body of Christ, it is an inescapable testimony to others that we are truly Christ's disciples.

This kind of love cannot be humanly manufactured or generated in the flesh. This kind of agape love can only be exercised as the believer is controlled by the Holy Spirit of God and therefore manifesting the spiritual fruit in Galatians 5:22–23 of which the very first is love. When we come to know Christ personally by grace through faith, we become the temple of the Holy Spirit. As Paul is talking about fleeing sexual immorality earlier in the book of First Corinthians, he says, "Or do you not know that your body is the temple of the Holy Spirit who is in you, whom you have from God, and you are not your own? For you were bought at a price; therefore glorify God in your body and in your spirit, which are God's" (1 Corinthians 6:19–20).

We were bought at a very high price. Through the incomparable sacrifice and shed blood of our Lord Jesus Christ on the cross our redemption was fully paid. Now our bodies and our spirits belong to Him. Now the Holy Spirit of God lives within us and our life work is to glorify God with both our bodies and our spirits. After salvation the new reality is, "I have been crucified with Christ; it is no longer I who live, but Christ lives in me; and the life which I now live in the flesh I live by faith in the Son of God, who loved me and gave Himself for me" (Galatians 2:20). "Therefore, if anyone is in Christ, he is a new creation; old things have passed away; behold, all things have become new" (2 Corinthians 5:17).

Though through salvation I have become the temple of the Holy Spirit, Christ lives within me, and I am a new creation in Him, the sad truth is I can still live with the flesh in control. This is why Paul said, "I say then: Walk in the Spirit, and you shall not fulfill the lust of the flesh. For the flesh lusts against the Spirit, and the Spirit against the flesh; and these are contrary to one another, so that you do not do the things that you wish" (Galatians 5:16–17).

Paul shares an important key here about living out who we truly are in Christ. We are to "walk" in the Spirit. This word *walk* is a continuous action word in the original language. It also is used in scripture to depict your journey in life or living your life. Therefore, we see Paul telling the Galatians to continuously live your life in the Spirit. "In the Spirit" here means to live under the control of and in obedience to the Holy Spirit of God. So, we are exhorted to continuously live our lives day to day in submission to and under the control of the Holy Spirit of God in order to not live out the lusts of the flesh. This is why Paul also said, "But put on the Lord Jesus Christ, and make no provision for the flesh, to fulfill its lusts" (Romans 13:14).

When we are not putting on the Lord Jesus Christ and living our lives in submission to and under the control of the Holy Spirit, we are making provisions for the flesh. We are opening the door, clearing the path, and carelessly leaving ourselves vulnerable for the flesh to be in control.

This was one of the main issues for the Corinthian Christians. They were still being controlled by the flesh. The first verses of chapter 3 in this book are a stinging rebuke of their carnality. Paul said, "And I, brethren, could not speak to you as to spiritual people but as to carnal, as to babes in Christ. I fed you with milk and not with solid food; for until now you were not able to receive it, and even now you are still not able; for you are still carnal. For where there are envy, strife, and divisions among you, are you not carnal and behaving like mere men?" (1 Corinthians 3:1–3).

The Corinthians were still living like mere men being controlled by the flesh. They were not living like new creations controlled by the Spirit. One of the main ways in which this fleshly control was manifested in their lives was apparently a lack of godly, self-sacrificial love in the misuse and abuse of their spiritual gifts, especially tongues. I say "especially tongues" because Paul very intentionally begins this chapter with tongues. Isn't it interesting that the only church in the New Testament we see Paul addressing this issue with is the church at Corinth? Dr. Zodhiates comments, "We have no record that this phenomenon occurred in any other New Testament church, nor did Paul ever seek to introduce it to them in his epistles. If this were the indispensable evidence of spirituality and the infilling of the Holy Spirit, we would certainly expect him to urge all believers to pray for this gift. Instead, he seeks to play it down among the Corinthians as much as possible" (Zodhiates 1983, 23).

In this famous chapter sometimes called the "love chapter," Paul begins by explaining that no matter what kind of action I take or sacrifice I make, no matter how great it may be considered by others, without godly love it profits nothing. He then moves into numerous definitions and character traits of true, godly love that seem to pinpoint many of the problems causing so much division and dysfunction at Corinth. Remember, the vitally important context of this discussion is dealing with the misuse and abuse of the spiritual gifts. He then speaks of other important spiritual functions within the Church coming to an end at some point. He concludes the chapter by giving them a lesson about putting away their childish things and growing up spiritually. Of the three things that remain—faith, hope, and love—he again drills the point home and proclaims that the greatest of them all is love.

The Priority of Love

(Abbreviations BC=Brief Commentary, SN=Study Notes)

13:1, BC—Paul says, "Even if I have the supernatural ability to speak with the tongues/languages of men and the tongues/languages of angels, if I do not have godly, sacrificial love as the motive behind those abilities, I really have no more impact than a loud gong or a clanging cymbal."

SN—In the first verses of this chapter, Paul is using very big, overarching statements in order to highlight his point concerning love. As you study these first few verses, it becomes clear Paul is using extremes as a teaching tool to help them see this priority of love. In light of the problems with spiritual gifts in the Church, it seems telling that he begins this discussion with tongues. Vincent comments, "Tongues. Mentioned first because of the exaggerated importance which the Corinthians attached to this gift" (Vincent 1985, 262). Dr. Lowery further explains the verse, "Paul's application of this and the following conditional clauses (1 Cor. 13:2–3) to himself was forceful since he could claim exceptional experiences, particularly in regard to the languages of men (14:18) and of angels (cf. 2 Cor. 12:4). But the statement was probably meant to include every imaginable mode of speech. It was a statement of hyperbole concerning exalted eloquence, which if void of love might be momentarily electrifying like a clash of gong or cymbal but then vanished just as quickly" (Walvoord and Zuck 1983, 535).

Dr. Patterson also addresses the use of these languages. "Paul simply suggested that if he were able to attain the use of such a lofty language or even if he were able by special spiritual intervention to speak all the languages of the tribes of the earth, he would still be nothing but a cacophony of sound unless he possessed love" (Patterson 1983, 230–231).

Obviously, Paul had the gift of tongues/languages, which he makes clear in 14:18. In this instance, at the beginning of chapter 13, he is using the illustration of this gift to the extreme as Dr. Patterson explains above. Paul uses the extreme, all-inclusive language in the following verses, such as "all mysteries," "all knowledge," "all faith," and "all my goods." Paul is explaining to them that if he were able to speak in every tongue/language known to man, without God's love he would just become noise. A reference to this noise may have also been familiar to the Corinthians from pagan rituals. "In NT times, rites honoring the pagan deities Cybele, Bacchus, and Dionysius included ecstatic noises accompanied by gongs, cymbals, and trumpets" (MacArthur 1997, 1750). The Nelson Study Bible also comments, "Paul uses an intentional exaggeration to illustrate the uselessness of each spiritual gift without love. The Corinthians would readily understand the images of sounding brass or a clanging cymbal, which is an allusion to pagan liturgy" (Radmacher 1997, 1932).

The word *though*, which begins this chapter in the King James Version and the New King James Version, also warrants mention. In many other translations, this Greek word is more accurately translated "if." Dr. Patterson addresses this word and says, "Though" is a highly questionable translation of the Greek term *ean*. A better translation would be, "If with the tongues of men and angels I should speak" (Patterson 1983, 230).

Greek native and scholar Dr. Spiros Zodhiates confirms this when he writes, "In the Greek, the verse begins with the hypothetical *ean*, which basically means "if (ever)" (Zodhiates 1983, 23).

Paul was not affirming here that he spoke every language known to man. A couple of other translations and paraphrases are helpful at this point.

"IF I [can] speak in the tongues of men and [even] of angels, but have not love [that reasoning, intentional, spiritual devotion such as is inspired by God's love for and in us], I am only a noisy gong or a clanging cymbal" (1 Corinthians 13:1, Amp.).

"If I could speak in any language in heaven or on earth but didn't love others, I would only be making meaningless noise like a loud gong or a clanging cymbal" (1 Corinthians 13:1, NLT).

"If I speak with the tongues of men and of angels, but do not have love, I have become a noisy gong or a clanging cymbal" (1 Corinthians 13:1, NASB).

Also in this verse, he mentions the tongues/languages of angels. This term warrants more discussion because it is referred to so frequently by those today who claim some kind of heavenly prayer language. Again, remember he is using extreme statements to make his point on love. Even if he was able to speak every conceivable language of men, and reaching to the extreme for emphasis, if he could even speak the exalted language of angels, which is the communication of heaven, without the love of God it becomes meaningless noise.

Paul is not affirming here that he speaks some angelic language or languages. He is using this statement as a vehicle of emphasis.

Interestingly, he says even if he could speak that language or languages, without God's love it would also be just noise.

Another instructive passage is Paul's record in 2 Corinthians 12 of the incredible vision he experienced when he was caught up into Paradise. He states in verse four that he, "heard inexpressible words, which it is not lawful for a man to utter" (2 Corinthians 12:4). The rendering of the New Living Translation is, ". . . was caught up into paradise and heard things so astounding that they cannot be told" (2 Corinthians 12:4, NLT).

Whether he was referring to some angelic/heavenly language here, we don't know. We do know that what he heard was inexpressible. We also know that even if he could express it somehow through some supernatural ability, he makes it extremely clear it was not lawful for a man to even express. Paul was forbidden from even trying to express it even if he had been able. Whatever the sounds were, they were reserved for heaven only and not some kind of heavenly, spiritual language God had given for the use of men.

It is also interesting to note that in many scriptural accounts where angels communicated with people, they spoke to them clearly in their own language. The angels, with whatever supernatural abilities God had given them, spoke to humans in their own human language so they would understand clearly what God wanted them to know. Some of these were the amazing, angelic communications that took place around the birth of Christ.

We also see Paul relating this phrase to himself. He said, "If I could speak." He didn't say, "If you could speak." He didn't say, "When you speak." He didn't say, "As you speak." He didn't say, "When the Holy Spirit enables you to speak." He is not in any way speaking of them having some heavenly, angelic prayer language. This phrase of scripture gives absolutely no recommendation to them about speaking some heavenly, angelic prayer language or further even affirming the possibility of speaking it. To claim that Paul gives some affirmation to the Corinthians or others of speaking in a heavenly language from this verse is reading something into the verse that is not there. "The theological word *eisegesis* is defined as, 'the interpretation of a text (as of the Bible) by reading into it one's own ideas'" (Woolf 1981, 361). This is an unfortunate but accurate description of what has been done too many times with this verse. This statement clearly related to him and was a vehicle to forcefully express his point of a lacking love.

Some of our charismatic friends have also claimed this wonderful, heavenly prayer language takes them to a higher level of intimacy and communication with the Lord. They sometimes rave about how it deepens and beautifies their relationship with the Lord as it never had been before. They speak of it as some kind of advanced spirituality that is not possible without this heavenly language. I believe they truly believe that is the case.

One of the things the book of First Corinthians makes very obvious is an immature spirituality, not some kind of advanced spirituality. This fact is inescapable as Paul said, "And I, brethren, could not speak to you as to spiritual people but *as to carnal, as to babes in Christ. I fed you with milk* and not with solid food; for until now *you were not able to receive it*, and even now you are *still not able*; for *you are still carnal*" (1 Corinthians 3:1–3a, emphasis added).

Paul continues after these verses speaking about the things in their lives that reveal their carnality and being controlled by the flesh. This church that seems to have practiced tongues more than any other church recorded in the New Testament certainly did not have an advanced spirituality according to Paul. Dr. Jerry Vines comments, "The practice of tongues-speaking provides no evidence for an advanced spirituality. Paul specifically says to the Corinthians, 'Brothers, I could not address you as spiritual but as worldly-mere infants in Christ' (1 Cor. 3:1). Tongues is never listed as some requirement or proof of the presence of the Holy Spirit or that one is at a higher level of spirituality" (Vines 1999, 92).

13:2, BC—Paul adds to the first point with even more extremes. And if I have prophetic powers and am able to understand all of the mysteries and I have all the knowledge and I possess all the faith so that I could even make mountains move with my faith, if I don't have God's love working in and through me, I am useless.

SN—Dr. Patterson speaks of the incredible nature of this verse. "This statement is staggering in its content. For one to be a prophet proclaiming the word of God, for one to know the mysteries of the kingdom of God and to have remarkable knowledge of the word and ways of God, further for one to be able to exercise mountain-moving faith, and even then consider himself a total failure is a remarkable affirmation" (Patterson 1983, 232).

Paul continues this barrage of extreme statements to highlight his point on love. It is remarkable the extent to which Paul goes to illustrate that God's love within us is the highest priority. We can possess all kinds of spiritual gifts with all that is included in them and still be useless without the all-important love of God indwelling us and flowing through us.

Most of the gifts in this verse have been discussed previously. However, Paul's statement about understanding all mysteries has not. Obviously, mysteries are those things that are hidden from man and impossible for him to know apart from supernatural intervention. Some of these mysteries of the kingdom of God are hidden until a certain point in time and then supernaturally revealed at God's chosen time. Other mysteries are permanently sealed for God alone. Some of these mysteries could also be connected to the gift of prophecy just mentioned. The main point of this verse is still the same as Paul says even if he knew all the mysteries of the kingdom of God, without God's love working in and through his life he would be nothing, or as the Amplified Bible puts it, "I am nothing—a useless nobody" (1 Corinthians 13:2, Amp.).

13:3, BC—And even if I give all of my material goods to feed the poor, and even if I go to the point of giving my body to be burned, if I do not have God's love working in and through me, then these sacrifices I make will not be any profit to me at all.

SN—Paul continues his extreme statements with the word *all*. He talks about what would be considered a very noble gesture by someone who considers himself or herself a Christian. He again directs it toward himself. If I were to gather up everything in my life that I own and literally bankrupt myself and then take all of the proceeds and use every penny of it to feed poor people, if I did this without God's love working in and through my life, there would be no profit to me. In addition, if I literally gave my body to be burned at the stake, without God's love working in and through my life, there would be no profit.

Paul's point couldn't be any clearer. So for the Corinthians, they needed to understand that the exercise of the spiritual gifts in and of themselves was not what was pleasing to God. God's desire was that His heart of love would be their heart.

The Characteristics of Love

13:4, BC—God's love is a love that is very patient and is known for its sweet spirit of kindness. God's love is a love that does not envy others and what they possess. God's love is a love that is humble, does not pridefully show off to others, and is not arrogant with a sense of superiority.

SN—Now Paul moves into a passage in which he begins to define and illustrate what God's love actually looks like. He first speaks of love as being very patient. It is long-suffering. It resists the temptation to jump into anger. This characteristic of love was lacking in the Corinthian Church, especially as it concerned their angry rush to take each other to court. This was something Paul mentioned as a terrible testimony in front of the civil authorities.

Paul next speaks of love as being kind. This was the sweet spirit of Christ that was the opposite of an angry spirit. Dr. Patterson actually quotes Dr. Zodhiates to define this word. "It denotes 'a grace that pervades and penetrates the whole nature, mellowing there all that would have been harsh and austere'" (Patterson 1983, 234). The lack of kindness also occurred in their angry responses to each other in court and in their actions in their Lord's Supper memorials.

Paul continues by saying that love does not envy. This seems to have been a particularly grievous lack of love within their church. Some members were very envious of the flashy, high-profile spiritual gifts God had given to others. They were jealous, which led to many other evidences of their lack of love.

Paul then says that real love does not parade itself. It is not boastful. Dr. A. T. Robertson explains, "Only here in N.T. and earliest known example. It means play the braggart" (Robertson 1931, 178). Real love is not boastful. On the other end of being jealous or envious of spiritual gifts, there was the problem of being boastful about them. Both of these problems were causing some of the divisions in the church.

Paul says real love is not puffed up. Dr. Robertson says this word means, "to puff oneself out like a pair of bellows" (Robertson 1931, 178). This is another facet of the boastful pride that is the opposite of true love. Much like some frogs that inflate their skin to enormous proportions as they are croaking, these Corinthians were inflated with pride to enormous proportions. Instead of the proper humility of love for God's amazing grace, they were using their gifts in an arrogant way, which caused divisions and jealousies.

13:5, BC—Real love does not act rudely toward others. It is not focused on seeking its own way. It is not easily provoked by others and chooses to not think evil things.

SN—Paul wanted them to know their rude behavior to one another was evidence of their carnality and lack of real love. Dr. Patterson writes, "Those concerned about possession of the gifts are reminded that when the gifts become hurtful and generate shameful or tactless behavior then the practitioners of those gifts are demonstrating the absence of adequate love" (Patterson 1983, 235).

Real love is not focused on seeking its own way. It is not out to promote "number one." Its focus is to help, encourage, give, lift up, and sacrifice for the good of others. This was especially needful with the Corinthians insisting on their own way. The book of Hebrews highlights this need as it exhorts, "And let us consider and give attentive, continuous care to watching over one another, studying how we may stir up (stimulate and incite) to love and helpful deeds and noble activities" (Hebrews 10:24, Amp.).

Real love is not easily provoked by others to angry outbursts and selfish behavior. It holds back and gives others the benefit of the doubt. This was also seemingly in short supply as the Corinthians lashed out at each other.

Real love chooses not to think evil thoughts toward others. This term speaks of keeping records in an account book. Vincent explains, "Love, instead of entering evil as a debt in its account book, voluntarily passes the sponge over what it endures (Godet)" (Vincent 1985, 265). Real love does not keep records concerning the wrongs others have done to them. The Corinthians were not only keeping records but actually going to court before the civil authorities to proclaim those records.

13:6, BC—Real love does not rejoice in evil things or unrighteous behavior. It rejoices in the truth of God's Word.

SN—Real love does not rejoice in things that are not pleasing to God. The Corinthians seemed to revel in some of these issues, such as divisiveness, selfishness, jealousy, and the misuse of spiritual gifts. They had formed their cliques and were standing against each other insisting on their own way. Paul speaks of these divisions in the first chapter when he says, "For it has been declared to me concerning you, my brethren, by those of Chloe's household, that there are contentions among you. Now I say this, that each of you says, 'I am of Paul,' or 'I am of Apollos,' or 'I am of Cephas,' or 'I am of Christ.' Is Christ divided? Was Paul crucified for you? Or were you baptized in the name of Paul?" (1 Corinthians 1:11–13). They were dividing up into groups following different leaders. It is sad that this is still a common practice I have seen many times through the years. It destroys the body dynamic of unity!

Real love rejoices in the truth of God's Word. It is humbly grateful for God's truth even when that truth is convicting and correcting. It finds joy in searching for and holding on to the treasure of God's truth.

13:7, BC—Real love is willing to bear the struggles of all things, believe the best through all things, hopes and trusts God for all things, and is willing to endure and persevere through all things.

SN—Paul continues to share the positive characteristics of real love. As opposed to the negative and selfish attitude of carnality, real love is positive in its approach. It is willing to bear the struggles and difficulties of life and sacrifice itself in order to manifest the compassionate love of God to others.

It also chooses to believe the best in various situations of life as opposed to being critical and believing the worst. It chooses to look on the bright side of things and trust God to work all things together for good.

It chooses to live in hope in all situations as opposed to living in gloom and fear. Love lives in hope and trusts in God. Without hope, you can't cope.

Love is willing to endure the trials and pains of life. It compassionately moves through every issue with a focus on the end of the race. When others are crushed and become bitter and controlled by the flesh, love continues to trust and move forward in faith. ". . . Let us lay aside every weight, and the sin which so easily ensnares us, and *let us run with endurance* the race that is set before us, looking unto Jesus, the author and finisher of our faith" (Hebrews 12:1–2, emphasis added).

The Eternal Nature of Love

13:8, BC—Real love will never fail or come to an end, but concerning prophecies they will come to an end, concerning tongues/

languages they will expire, concerning knowledge it will also come to an end.

SN—In pointing to the superiority of love, Paul says love is unending. It is eternal in its nature just as God is eternal. It will never fail and will never come to an end. Though other gifts are temporal in nature and will end at some point, love is eternal and enduring.

There is no question that these three coveted spiritual gifts will end, as is made clear in these verses. The real question that is surrounded by so much controversy and debate is, when will the end of these gifts occur? What is the ending time frame Paul is speaking of?

It is needful and instructive to look at the original language as it concerns this issue. Interestingly the gifts of prophecy and knowledge mentioned here by Paul have a connection with the Greek word used to describe their ending. Dr. Patterson explains, "The words translated 'fail' and 'vanish away' are actually the same word. It's lexical form (*katargeo*) means 'to render useless or make inoperative.' Prophecies are said 'to fail,' not in the sense that they prove untrue, but rather in the sense that they will simply no longer be necessary. The same is true of the partial knowledge believers possess at the present time. That knowledge shall be far surpassed since 'then shall I know even as also I am known' (v. 12). The gift of knowledge will have fallen into uselessness" (Patterson 1983, 238).

After seeing this connection with prophecy and knowledge and the Greek word that describes their ending, we now need to carefully look at the word used to describe the ending time frame of tongues/languages. It is a very different word with a different description of its ending. Dr. W. A. Criswell gives us a careful explanation of the difference in these words and their meaning. "When Paul comes to speak of tongues in 1 Corinthians 13:8, he not only changes the verb but he also changes the voice of the verb he uses. As with 'prophecies' and as with 'knowledge' we would have expected him to use the future passive *katargethesontai*. Not so. He uses a different verb, *pauo*, 'to cause to cease,' and he changes the voice from passive to middle, *pausontai*, which literally translated means, 'tongues shall make themselves to cease,' or 'tongues shall automatically cease of themselves.' Phillip's translation of the verse goes like this: 'If there are prophecies they will be fulfilled and done with, if there are 'tongues' the need for them will disappear, if there be knowledge it will be swallowed up in truth" (Criswell 1966, 177).

So what we see here is that Paul clearly used a different word to describe the ending of the gift of tongues as opposed to the word used for these other two gifts. Whatever else might be said, there is a clear distinction drawn between the descriptive endings. Now that we have confirmed the tongues mentioned here has a different description of its ending, we need to assess the ways in which that different ending can be applied, which we will address in the next couple verses.

13:9, BC—While we are still in this world, our knowledge is limited and reveals only a part of God's plan for us. Also, as we prophesy we understand that it too is limited and is only a part of God's omniscient design.

SN—As Paul continues to compare the eternal nature of true love and the temporal nature of these spiritual gifts, he adds another layer of contrast. Not only will these spiritual gifts end at some point, they are limited even now while we use them. These spiritual gifts that have been given so much prominence are only partial in nature. They do not reveal to us God's whole and complete plan.

13:10, BC—But when God's perfect, whole, and complete plan has been ushered in, then all of these things, which only give a partial, incomplete view, will be done away with and ended.

SN—It is needful at this point to have a more comprehensive discussion of this verse and its meaning. We need to carefully examine how "that which is perfect" will bring an end to these spiritual gifts that are only partial in nature. There has been much debate concerning what "that which is perfect" actually means. There have been several prominent possibilities promoted and written about by theologians of different persuasions.

The first possible definition of "that which is perfect" is the New Testament scriptures. This is actually the definition I was taught in seminary many years ago. This definition declares that these spiritual gifts were purposed for and most needed during the beginning era of the New Testament Church when the scriptures had not yet been completed. Upon the completion of the New Testament scriptures, which are referred to as, "that which is perfect," these spiritual gifts were no longer needed.

The second possible definition of "that which is perfect" is the Rapture of the Church. This definition declares that when Christ comes to snatch the Church away, these spiritual gifts will no longer be needed. The coming of "that which is perfect" refers to Christ coming in the clouds and the Body of Christ being caught up with Him as recorded in 1 Thessalonians 4:17.

The third possible definition of "that which is perfect" is the final, eternal, heavenly state. This definition declares that after all of God's purposes have been accomplished, the Second Coming, the millennial reign, all of His judgments, the abolishing of all His enemies, and the ushering in of the final, eternal, heavenly state that these spiritual gifts will no longer be needed.

Dr. Patterson addresses these three views. "The problem with the first view is that while the Scripture is perfect in all that it affirms, its perfection lies in its errorlessness—not in its completeness. God has told us in the Scriptures all that we need to know for a successful life and a certain eternity. He has given us much more besides. Nevertheless, it remains that 'Eye hath not seen nor ear heard, neither have entered into the heart of man the things which God hath prepared for them that love Him' (2:9). At present we at best see through a mirror darkly. Therefore, it is unlikely that 'that which is perfect' refers to the Bible.

"The second view, while certainly presenting one who is perfect in the coming of Jesus, is still probably a faulty view in that conditions will not yet be perfect. Even during the millennial age with all the blessings of that era, when Satan is loosed at its conclusion (Rev. 20:7–8), he will have an immediate following from among those who have outwardly submitted to the rule of God during the thousand-year reign of Christ but inwardly have never been regenerated.

"Therefore, 'that which is perfect' is probably best construed as a reference to the eternal state of the believer's existence in heaven with God. That is the only time, in fact, which suits the condition, 'then that which is in part shall be done away'" (Patterson 1983, 239–240).

The first view, which believes that the completed New Testament scriptures are "that which is perfect" has some problems. Even after the completion of the New Testament scriptures, we still have need of spiritual insight and knowledge concerning the scriptures. We also still have need of the spiritual gifting from God to continue to proclaim the Word of God. These two spiritual gifts are still in operation in the church age today. In stating that the New Testament scriptures are not "that which is perfect," Dr. McArthur says, "The Scriptures do not allow us to see 'face-to-face' or have perfect knowledge as God does (v. 12)" (MacArthur 1997, 1750).

When Paul says we are only able to see as through a mirror dimly and that our spiritual understanding is only partial, it is hard to see the New Testament scriptures here as the true definition of "that which is perfect" bringing an end to the need for these spiritual gifts. In other words, things are not perfect yet in its fullest sense to be able to render these spiritual gifts inoperative.

The second view, which believes the Rapture of the Church by Christ constitutes "that which is perfect" also has some problems. Even after the Rapture has occurred, wherever you place that event in reference to the seven years of tribulation, it is still followed by the thousand-year millennial reign of Christ. This presents a major problem when considering that this millennial reign will have its own preachers and teachers. Dr. McArthur states, "The 'perfect' is not the rapture of the church or the second coming of Christ, since the kingdom to follow these events will have an abundance of preachers and teachers (cf. Is. 29:18, 32:3,4; Joel 2:28; Rev. 11:3)" (MacArthur 1997, 1750).

Not only will there be an abundance of preachers and teachers after the Rapture, but there is also the related problem of a spiritual rebellion toward the end of this millennial reign that reveals it is not perfect.

With the preachers and teachers who will obviously be ministering with spiritual gifting in that time frame after the Rapture and the spiritual rebellion that will happen, it seems very difficult to think of the Rapture as "that which is perfect" that will completely abolish the need for the spiritual gifts of knowledge and prophecy.

This leaves us with the third view concerning "that which is perfect." This view sees it as most accurately represented by the heavenly eternal state. Only when time as we know it has come to an end and all rebellion has been abolished and consigned to its eternal holding place can we truly say that the "perfect" has fully come. Then we will have "face-to-face" perfect knowledge without any imperfect factors to interfere. The perfection of knowledge will sit on the throne of heaven eternally. Then that which is partial and incomplete will truly be no more.

Now we move on to the issue of tongues/languages and how they will be ended. As we confirmed earlier, this spiritual gift of tongues/languages is ended in a different way than the gifts of prophecy and knowledge. Remember, the Greek word used to speak of the gift of tongues/languages coming to an end was a word that meant "tongues shall make themselves to cease," or "tongues shall automatically cease of themselves." From this meaning, Phillips translates the phrase, "if there are 'tongues' the need for them will disappear" (Criswell 1966, 177). This is quite different from the gifts of prophecy and knowledge that end by the coming of "that which is perfect." Nothing will act upon the gift of tongues/languages as with these other two gifts to bring them to an end. The tongues/languages will automatically cease of themselves at the point in time when God's purpose for them has been fulfilled. Dr. Patterson explains, "This is, of course, precisely what we have recorded for us in the New Testament. Once the gospel has been authenticated through the use of tongues on the Day of Pentecost (once again understood in its Acts reference to be an instance of a language never before formally studied being spoken for the purpose of communicating the gospel) and extended to the Gentiles in the home of Cornelius in Acts 10 and the strange case of the disciples who had known only the baptism of John in Ephesus (Acts 19:1–6), there is no further mention of tongues except in this extended discussion in 1 Corinthians" (Patterson 1983, 240).

This was a wonderful, spiritual gift given by God at Pentecost to clearly communicate His words to people of other languages and to astonish and impact them in order to prove/authenticate that this was God. With all of the scores of false gods and false prophets trying to persuade people to follow them, God was making sure there would be no mistaking the supernatural power of God behind this new way of God's grace through faith in Jesus Christ. God used it to serve His purposes in initiating this new direction, and it definitely had the desired effect.

To further confirm its temporary nature in the purposes of God, Dr. W. A. Criswell expounds upon where it is found and where it is not. "1 Corinthians is one of Paul's earliest letters. It is preceded only by the two epistles to the church at Thessalonica. After Paul wrote 1 Corinthians, he wrote 2 Corinthians, but in this latter epistle he never refers to speaking in tongues. After Paul wrote 1 Corinthians, he wrote a letter to the churches of Galatia, but he never refers to tongues. After Paul wrote 1 Corinthians, he wrote the letter to the church at Rome, but he never refers to speaking in tongues. After Paul wrote 1 Corinthians, he wrote Philippians, and Colossians, and Philemon, and Ephesians, and the Pastoral Epistles of 1 Timothy and Titus and 2 Timothy, but in none of them does he ever mention speaking in tongues. Tongues is the first sign-gift that ceased" (Criswell 1966, 178).

It is clear as we study these other books written by the apostle Paul that there are numerous spiritual problems and needs he addresses. Paul is teaching them how to grow in their intimacy with God and how to be a true soldier of Jesus Christ. He is teaching them how to stand strong against the enemy. He is teaching them who they are in Christ and how to stand in that authority. He especially teaches Timothy, his son in Christ, to "preach the word" and live in such a way that he fulfills God's purposes in his life, but he never says a word to him in these letters inspired by the Holy Spirit of God Himself about speaking in tongues. How can that possibly be?

This is a gift that God gave and God used. God had a purpose, and His purpose was accomplished. He revealed His purposeful power at Pentecost and clearly authenticated the new church era in its beginning stage. After God's purpose was accomplished in the beginning stage of the New Testament Church, the gift of tongues/languages ceased automatically of itself, as defined by the original word *cease*, and no recorded mention of it is ever seen again in any of the other New Testament books. To claim that this gift is an ongoing part of God's design for the Church when there is zero mention of it in any other New Testament Church letter other than this troubled, immature church being scolded for misuse and abuse is untenable. That Paul wants them to move forward out of their spiritual immaturity and fascination with certain spiritual gifts is undeniable in the verse that follows.

13:11, BC—Back when I was a child, the way I spoke and my ability to speak was like that of a child. The way that I perceived things and understood them was like a child. My thinking and thought processes were also like a child, but when I became a full-grown man, I stopped doing things in childish ways.

SN—Paul now begins a strong exhortation to grow up. He begins by sharing several things that relate to childhood and immaturity. These three things that illustrate Paul's point are the way he spoke as a child, the way he understood as a child, and the way he thought as a child. His way of speaking, understanding, and thinking were childish and immature. Obviously, he is using these three things in particular to address specific points of spiritual need in the Corinthians' lives.

It is very interesting to me that the very first point he makes in this verse about immaturity concerns the way he spoke. The immaturity of a child is revealed in what they speak, how they speak, and the attitude with which they speak. All of these were being addressed by Paul as a problem. The content of what they were speaking along with the timing and emotional nature of how they were speaking and the fleshly attitudes with which they were speaking were all evidences of the spiritual immaturity Paul is highlighting.

He says, "When I became a mature adult, I made a conscious decision to put away those childish ways of speaking, understanding, and thinking." He is admonishing them to make a conscious decision to leave the ways of childish immaturity and move forward into spiritual maturity. All of the division he begins to speak about, even in the first chapter of this book, along with the bickering, envy, jealousy, pride, and immorality, he characterizes as childish immaturity. He wants them to see the error of this and the damaging testimony of this immaturity to others. Dr. Patterson writes, "The implication is amply clear. The Corinthians in the excitement of their beginning walk with Christ had reveled in spiritual gifts, particularly those that were more sensational and had greater appeal to their emotional desires. Now they must proceed to maturity, putting away childish things and becoming Christian men" (Patterson 1983, 241).

13:12, BC—The way we are able to see spiritual things right now is blurry and dim, but the time is coming when we will see with perfect clarity as we are face-to-face with Christ. The spiritual things I understand now are only part of a complete understanding, but when I am with Christ face-to-face, I will possess that complete knowledge just as I am completely known.

SN—Paul draws a contrast between our spiritual understanding now and our spiritual understanding in eternity with God. He illustrates our limited spiritual understanding by using a mirror. The Roman mirrors of that time were drastically different from the amazing, crystal-clear mirrors we enjoy today. Dr. A. T. Robertson comments on the mirror and the original Greek word used for "darkly/dimly." "Ancient mirrors were of polished metal, not glass, those in Corinth being famous. *Darkly (en ainigmati)*. Literally, in an enigma" (Robertson 1931, 179).

Not only was the current spiritual understanding like trying to see your reflection in a piece of polished metal, but it was also dark, which only added to the sight impairment. Even with inspired scripture and the gifts of prophecy and knowledge, our spiritual understanding is partial at best when compared to what is coming.

Then Paul adds the contrast of the glorious time when we are no longer looking in an imperfect mirror but directly into the face of God Himself. When we are face-to-face with perfect sight of our perfect God, then the imperfect sight as though in a mirror will be gone forever. Paul is saying, "Right now my spiritual sight is partial and imperfect but when that glorious face-to-face moment arrives, then I will have complete knowledge in glory just as I am also completely and perfectly known."

13:13, BC—And now these Christian graces will continue and endure. They are faith, hope, and love and these three will abide forever, but the greatest of them all is love.

SN—Paul has very skillfully communicated the beauty and priority of true love. Within the context of this very passage, he has addressed many of the spiritual problems within the Corinthian Church. Their lack of love as manifested by many regarding their behaviors and actions are laid bare by the true characteristics and behaviors of agape love. The contrast of human love to God's love is simply stated by Stuart Briscoe when he said, "Human love says, 'I will love you if . . .' God says, 'I will love you even . . .'" (McHenry 2001, 168).

Paul concludes this beautiful passage with a simple but poignant reminder of his theme. Though the spiritual gifts given to the Church are all temporary, there are three graces/virtues that will last forever. The Summarized Bible concludes, "Love alone can give value to any service rendered in Christ's name, and it is therefore the supreme gift of the Spirit, to be coveted and prayed for above all others. Faith trusts and appropriates, hope expects, but love expresses Christ and blesses men" (Brooks 1975, 253).

A Picture of Love

A picture of love she was to me, that beautiful smile, that wonderful glee
Always a warm and loving embrace, always a kiss upon my face

Teaching me love by action and deed, teaching me care whatever the need
Never a hint of meanness or fear, only a wealth of comfort and cheer

Showing the life of Jesus her Lord, firmly attached by salvation's strong cord
Living her life with meaning and grace, trusting her Lord whatever the case

Wonderful wife and mother and friend, thinking of others to life's very end
Leaving a legacy filled with God's love, filled up
from treasures in heaven above

Touching a little boy all his life long, memories that fill his heart with a song
You were a picture of what life could be, you were a picture of love to me.

Written for my grandma, Mildred Hyskell, at her homegoing celebration
With much love, Mark D. Hyskell November 1, 2001

Chapter 7
The Big Caution

1 Corinthians 14
Follow God's Design

Now that Paul has addressed the terrible dysfunction and disunity in chapter 12 and the lack of true love in chapter 13, he moves on to deal with the misuse and misunderstandings concerning tongues in chapter 14.

Chapter 14 is the final linchpin in this triad of scolding correctives. The whole chapter seems to be a cautionary instructive on how to correct the misuse and abuse specifically of tongues. It becomes evident with practically the whole chapter dedicated to this issue that the gift of tongues had taken on an inordinate place of prominence within the group of spiritual gifts given to the Church. Due to the carnal nature of the Corinthians that still seemed to be dominating their lives, the gift of tongues had been elevated to an improper level that was actually destructive to the spiritual health of the church.

Remember that the fleshly control within their lives is glaringly evident in Paul's letter and was having a disastrous effect not only on the exercise of the spiritual gifts, but of their testimony to their lost city as well. That the carnal nature of the Corinthians was still dominating their lives currently as Paul wrote is evidenced in many places, but none more clearly than the immorality addressed in chapter 5. Paul spoke of the sexual immorality that had been reported within the church family. It is such gross immorality that Paul states, ". . . and such sexual immorality as is not even named among the Gentiles—that a man has his father's wife!" (1 Corinthians 5:1).

He is addressing the situation of a young man actually living with and having sexual relations with (most likely) his stepmother. Not only does this incestuous relationship by a member of the Corinthian Church draw Paul's rebuke but also the refusal of the church family to do anything about it. There was no mourning or remorse from the church family over this sinful behavior and its destructive influence. There was no action of any kind to address the problem. The mere acceptance of this kind of immorality that was so prevalent within the city was a shocking proof of the spiritual condition of these members.

This kind of spiritual degradation cannot be neatly compartmentalized. It cannot be kept completely contained just as one ingredient mixed into a recipe cannot be contained by itself. This is why Paul went on to speak about the leaven affecting the whole recipe in chapter 5. "Do you not know that a little leaven leavens the whole lump?" (1 Corinthians 5:6).

This effect of spiritual corruption becomes mixed with and permeates the whole body either directly or indirectly by their testimony to the world. It seems many Christians in our day try to exercise these spiritual gifts with a perspective that is completely divorced from any understanding of these serious spiritual problems Paul is addressing. Many times, with the best of intentions, the Corinthians were running after these gifts with no regard for the serious spiritual problems that were surrounding them in this most famous of all gifts passage. These people were misusing spiritual gifts while being compromised spiritually.

Paul begins this chapter by basically saying, "Do this; don't do that." He is contrasting the use of prophecy as opposed to tongues. He is strongly exhorting them to prioritize the use of prophecy and not tongues. He is encouraging them to use clear communication people will understand as opposed to, "speaking into the air." He continues to speak of the need to use their spiritual gifts for the edification of the whole Body of Christ. In regard to understanding communication within the church body, Paul says he would rather "speak five words with my understanding, that I may teach others also, than ten thousand words in a tongue" (1 Corinthians 14:19).

He speaks of the gift of tongues causing unbelievers to think you are insane as opposed to the gift of prophecy, causing them to be convinced, convicted, and worship God.

He asks, "How is it that when you come together that each of you are caught up in your own spiritual world individually instead of following God's design to do everything for the edification of the Body?" He then follows up by giving definitive guidelines on how to properly use the gifts if at all. He then speaks of the role of women within this context of spiritual gifts and ends the chapter with a rather telling admonition to, "Let all things be done decently and in order" (1 Corinthians 14:40).

The whole chapter is permeated with the feeling of a father scolding his children for their immature behavior. He is saying, "Let this be your desire. Move in this direction; don't move in that direction. Do what is best for everyone. Do this, but don't do that. Why are you doing that? Follow these guidelines instead of what you've been doing, and let everything be done with godly honor and order." These immature Corinthians and their use of spiritual gifts were most certainly not a model to emulate, but rather to avoid. This is the context of thought as we study this important chapter.

God's Design Is for Edification

(Abbreviations BC=Brief Commentary, SN=Study Notes)

14:1, BC—It is my desire that you pursue love as the main priority and desire to use your spiritual gifts, but my strongest desire is that you would put a priority on exercising the spiritual gift of prophecy.

SN—Though some commentators believe the first part of verse 1 belongs at the end of chapter 13, the wonderful truth of pursuing love as the highest priority retains its impact in either place. After the beautiful exposition on love in chapter 13, it actually seems fitting that this theme would be the opening umbrella of thought over all of the cautionary thoughts to follow.

Obviously, the Corinthians had proven from their immature behavior that they had an inordinate obsession with the exercise of the spiritual gifts, and tongues was at the top of the list. In his attempt to encourage a proper balance, Paul wants them to run after love and while running after love to desire to use their spiritual gifts in the proper way. Then he intentionally points their direction away from tongues and toward prophecy. He wanted their greatest desire to be pointed toward prophecy, which would edify the whole Body of Christ as opposed to tongues, which would not.

14:2, BC—The one who speaks in a tongue does not speak for the good of and edification of men but only to God. No one around him can even understand anything he is saying. What is really happening is that in the spirit, he is speaking mysterious things that are unknown.

SN—As we begin to study this verse and the remainder of this chapter, we need to lay some foundational groundwork for a correct understanding. It is critically important for us to know the correct meanings of words and therefore how they give meaning to the whole. Without an understanding of the correct meanings behind the words *tongue* and *tongues*, our perception and even our theology is blurred. Dr. Patterson speaks of three main positions concerning the meanings of *tongue* and *tongues* as they are used in this chapter.

The first position believes every occurrence of the words *tongue* and *tongues* in this chapter refers to what we would call ecstatic utterance. They believe these words are clearly not the supernatural ability to speak a known human language, which you have never studied. They hold that these words referred to a kind of supernatural, heavenly language beyond human language.

The second position believes the use of these words in this chapter refer to the spiritual gift of tongues/languages as used in Acts chapter 2. They refuse the proposition that these words were referring to some kind of ecstatic utterance whereby people spoke in unintelligible sounds. They believe all the uses of these words refer to the tongues/languages as seen at Pentecost.

The third position believes the use of these words in this chapter refer to two different kinds of "tongues." They do not believe it is possible for all the uses of these words to refer exclusively to either ecstatic utterance or to a known human language that had never been studied by the speaker. They believe reference is made to both of these meanings within the chapter as Paul tries to delineate what is accurate and useful to the whole Body and what is not accurate and is useful only to the individual.

I must confess, after studying this issue for many years in seminary and as a young pastor, I was still troubled. As I read the verses of chapter 14, some of these verses seemed to be clearly speaking of some kind of ecstatic utterance or unintelligible sounds that no one could understand as in verse 2. On the other hand, it also seemed just as clear some of these verses were speaking of unlearned human languages spoken as a gift from God to share His Word with people of many different nationalities and languages such as in Paul's life in verse 18. I struggled to see how an honest rendering of these words could be construed as the first position or second position exclusively, and further how this seeming dilemma could be resolved with a definitive interpretation.

In the 80s, as I was doing undergraduate and then graduate work in seminary, God blessed me with teaching from many great men, two of which were Dr. Spiros Zodhiates whom I sat under for some classes and Dr. Paige Patterson whom I studied under at the Criswell College in Dallas, Texas. God used both of these men and their writings in my life to help resolve this dilemma in 1 Corinthians 14. When I met with Dr. Paige in his office one day, he gave me a copy of his book, *The Troubled Triumphant Church*, which is an expositional commentary on 1 Corinthians. His scholarly approach and careful exposition opened up to me this third position mentioned above, which is also the position held by Dr. Zodhiates. The light of comprehension came on for me and my struggle with this point was over.

This third position on the use of "tongue" and "tongues" in this passage made spiritual sense. I knew Paul had the spiritual gift of tongues/languages as in Acts chapter 2, and God clearly used him to reach multitudes of people all over the known world. I also knew in some of these verses Paul was addressing something that was clearly not the tongues/languages of Acts chapter 2. Now it all made sense, and there was a spark of spiritual excitement about this clear answer for which I had struggled so long. As I studied the chapter with this new understanding in mind, Paul's attempt to correct their immature misuse and abuse of the spiritual gift came into clear view. In some verses, Paul was addressing the ecstatic utterances, which were the Corinthians' imitation of the real gift, stemming from their immature and inordinate desires. In other verses, Paul was addressing the original gift of tongues/languages as in Acts chapter 2.

As Paul addresses their use of ecstatic utterance in some verses, it seems to be marked by a lack of comprehension and understanding by anyone hearing it as in verse 2. Their ecstatic utterance is also marked by a self-centered acquisition as opposed to the edification of the whole Body of Christ as is seen in verse 4. These ecstatic utterance features were clearly not part of God's design.

As Paul addresses the use of tongues/languages (as in Acts chapter 2) in other verses, it seems to be presented as generally inferior to the gift of prophecy as in verses 5 and 39. Paul also places definitive and severe guidelines on this gift in his attempt to stop the corporate chaos as is seen in verses 27 and 28.

With these understandings, we return to the text of verse 2. Paul says the one speaking in a tongue does not speak to men but to God because no one can understand him. As we contrast this tongue with the tongues of Acts chapter 2, we see the dramatic differences. At Pentecost, those who had been given the gift of tongues/languages spoke specifically to the people who were there in the city. In this instance of a tongue in 1 Corinthians 14:2, the person speaking with a tongue is not speaking to any human. At Pentecost in Acts chapter 2, the opposite is true. When they used the gift of tongues/languages at Pentecost, they spoke clearly in the known, human languages of all the nationalities present, and they clearly understood the message of the wonderful works of God. In this instance in 1 Corinthians 14:2, there is no understanding on the part of anyone around. At Pentecost in Acts chapter 2, the gift of tongues/languages was used to speak to people only. In this use of a tongue in 1 Corinthians 14:2, the gift was used to speak to God only. This is, of course, with the understanding that only an omniscient God could make any kind of sense out of unintelligible sounds. Obviously in this verse we are studying in 14:2, Paul is not dealing with the Acts chapter 2 gift of tongues/languages but rather with the Corinthian imitation that had become so prevalent in their rush to exercise gifts.

The verse concludes with the phrase, "in the spirit he speaks mysteries." Though this phrase has been misconstrued to mean he was speaking some kind of mysteries of God in the power of the Holy Spirit, the context and the overview of the misuse of gifts Paul is dealing with paints a different picture. Dr. Zodhiates addresses this issue as he writes, "No one understands incoherent sounds, runs the argument, and therefore he is speaking mysteries in the spirit. The word 'spirit' does not refer to the Holy Spirit here, but to the spirit of the one speaking. Verse 14 makes this absolutely indisputable, because the possessive pronoun 'my' (*mou*) is used and also the definite article 'the' (*to*). 'For if I pray in an unknown tongue, my spirit prayeth, but my understanding is unfruitful.' The literal Greek is 'the spirit mine'" (Zodhiates 1983, 67).

As Paul addresses this Corinthian imitation, which we have already seen is clearly different than the Acts chapter 2 languages, he is saying the spirit of the speaker is speaking mysterious things. It is not a Holy Spirit-inspired mystery wherein the truth of God is revealed after being hidden; rather, they are unintelligible sounds generated from the spirit of the speaker. The New American Standard Bible renders it, "but in his spirit he speaks mysteries" (1 Corinthians 14:2, NASB). It is another example of the fascination and overindulgence of the Corinthians toward the use of gifts.

14:3, BC—But on the other hand, he who prophesies—the one who proclaims the truths of God's Word in the power of the Holy Spirit—actually teaches, edifies, encourages, and stimulates and is a source of comfort to them.

SN—As we see all throughout this passage, Paul continually prioritizes the gift of prophecy as opposed to tongues. This verse is a follow-up to the previous verse to emphasize the superiority of prophecy. He then delineates several very important elements of the gift of prophecy. The first element he uses to describe the benefits of prophecy is edification. This is also a word used numerous times in this context and is so frequently referred to that it merits defining. Dr. Patterson explains, "The word is made up of *oikos*, meaning 'house,' and *domeo*, meaning 'to build'; hence, the concept of the building of a house is conveyed by the expression. This sense is observable in the fact that in English we frequently refer to a building as an 'edifice.' 'Edification,' therefore, means the construction of a serviceable and helpful unit. Biblical preaching when heard and obeyed will inevitably result in the construction of a serviceable unit of life for the listener" (Patterson 1983, 247).

So Paul says prophecy edifies and builds up the Body of Christ, but it also includes exhortation and comfort. The exhortation was a provocative stimulation to live out the truths of God's Word. The comfort includes the great assurance from God's Word that He is Almighty and that our lives and eternity are in His hands. This was the positive priority Paul desired for the Corinthians instead of the fascination with tongues.

14:4, BC—The one who speaks in a tongue builds up himself, but the one who prophesies—proclaims the truths of God's Word in the power of the Holy Spirit—builds up the Church.

SN—Paul now draws the head-to-head contrast from the theme of these first several verses. The one who speaks in a tongue is acquiring something out of it for himself or herself only. Again, this is clearly not the gift of tongues/languages given by God to be used only when the Church could receive edification. The spiritual gifts of God were not given solely for the individual member of the Body of Christ any more than the eye is given the ability of sight solely for the good of the eye only. Then Paul draws the stark contrast by saying, "But he who prophesies edifies the church." This gift of prophecy was a giving gift. It was a gift that built up, encouraged, and comforted the whole Body of Christ.

14:5, BC—I wish you all were gifted with the ability to speak in tongues/languages, but my greater desire is that you would have the spiritual gifting to prophesy because the one who prophesies is superior to the one who speaks in tongues/languages, unless he interprets those languages so the whole church may receive edification.

SN—In the context of this verse, Paul uses the plural "tongues" to refer to the gift of tongues/languages as in Acts chapter 2.

First, we need to address the first phrase in which Paul says he wishes they were all gifted with the ability to speak in tongues/languages. Several things are very obvious from his previous teaching on spiritual gifts. One is that these gifts are distributed by God's design and plan for His purposes to be accomplished within the Body of Christ. The spiritual gifts are not chosen by the individuals but given only as God chooses. Another obvious teaching from Paul is they are supposed to humbly and gratefully use their gifts for the good of the whole Body. They are not to covet the spiritual gifts of others and allow jealousy and envy to cause disunity. With this context in mind, it is clear Paul is speaking hypothetically concerning this wish.

Second, we need to address the contrast of the verse itself. This wish concerning the gift of tongues/languages is, once again, contrasted with the gift of prophecy. In other words, though it would be great if you were all spiritually gifted with the gift of tongues/languages (though we know this is not literally the case from 12:30), it would be even greater if you have the spiritual gift of prophecy (though we know all of them did not literally have this gift either from 12:29).

This theme of contrast between the two gifts is then explained. The one who prophesies—who proclaims the truth of God's Word in the power of the Holy Spirit—is superior to the one who speaks in tongues/languages, unless he also interprets the language so that the whole church can receive edification. Even when this genuine gift of tongues/languages was exercised in this beginning phase of the church, it was inferior to prophecy except in the instance where the speaker gives a clear and accurate interpretation of God's words with the specific intention of edifying and building up the whole Body of Christ.

With Paul speaking of the superiority of prophecy over the gift of tongues/languages and then adding the phrase, "unless indeed he interprets, that the church may receive edification," it leaves one wondering exactly why he added this final phrase. Perhaps this was part of the Corinthians' problem with which he was trying to deal. Perhaps even those who were using the legitimate gift of tongues/languages were misusing the gift in their passionate immaturity by being caught up in the gift itself without giving any required interpretation for the good of the whole Body.

God's Design Is for Understanding

14:6, BC—And now my brothers and sisters in Christ, if I did come to you speaking with tongues/languages, how would I be of any help to you unless I speak to you in a clear communication by revelation, by knowledge, by prophesying, or by teaching?

SN—This whole section of scripture is speaking of clear communication and how to have a clear understanding of that clear communication as is especially evident in the following verses. It seems evident from Paul's continual focus on the edification of the whole Body that the Corinthians were misusing the gift for selfish purposes. Even the genuine gift of tongues/languages when used without any interpretation gave no edification to the church and fell short of its purpose.

Paul has just finished in the previous verse speaking to them of the absolute necessity of a clear interpretation of tongues/languages in order to be useful and edifying to the church. Without that clear interpretation, Paul said the gift was inferior when contrasted with prophecy and later in this chapter even prohibits its use in verse 28.

After mentioning this clear requirement for interpretation in order to have clear communication and edification, Paul now asks a question. "If I come to you speaking in tongues/languages, what benefit is that going to be to you without a clear understanding of what I am saying? Unless there is an interpretation to enable clear understanding and edification of the church as I just told you to do, how would that be of benefit to the whole Body? How would I even be able to help you unless there is an interpretation and you receive a clear, understandable communication by revelation, knowledge, prophesying, or teaching?"

14:7, BC—Even material objects without any life in them, like musical instruments such as the flute or harp, when a sound is produced through them, unless there is a distinction in the sounds that distinguishes them as different or separate notes or tones, how will anyone be able to understand the music that is piped or played?

SN—Paul continues to address this matter of clear understanding and comprehension, especially within this context of tongues. Now he uses two musical instruments to illustrate the problem with tongues, especially as practiced by the Corinthians. He speaks of the flute and harp and makes a point of saying they are material objects without life. Even material objects without life can make this point about the necessity of clarity and understanding. If a person plays these musical instruments by continuously making sounds with no recognizable distinctions in notes or tones, then no one will be able to distinguish an understandable song or have any idea what they are playing. It then becomes nothing more than noise without any enjoyment or enrichment to anyone listening.

14:8, BC—For if the trumpet used to give a specific signal to the people of an approaching enemy gives an uncertain, ambiguous, indefinite sound, how would the people know to begin preparing for battle?

SN—Paul presses the point even further now concerning a lack of clarity and understanding. This time he uses the illustration of a trumpet played clearly and specifically in very certain tones to give clear and specific signals to the people or military. Now the lack of clarity and understanding could have a disastrous and even deadly effect. The people without their clear signal could be taken completely by surprise without even being able to defend themselves. The critical need demands a clear signal. In the same way, we have a critical need for spiritual truth from our God to be able to defend against the enemy, and without clarity and understanding the result can be disastrous.

14:9, BC—In the same way, I want you to understand, unless you speak with your tongue words that are easy to understand and have clarity for the hearer, how will they be able to know and understand the message you have spoken? If they have no understanding of your message, you will just be speaking meaningless, ineffectual sounds out into the air.

SN—Paul now takes these illustrations with the musical instruments and relates them to the Corinthians' spiritual communications. He begins with the phrase, "so likewise you." Just as these instruments must play the notes with distinction and clarity in order to be understood, the Corinthians must speak words with distinction and clarity. If your words are not easy to understand for the listeners, then how will they have any comprehension of God's message? Without the understanding of the audience, the spiritual gift has been misused and you are speaking sounds out into the air, which produce no edification. Speaking these sounds out into the air doesn't help anyone.

14:10, BC—There are, in reality, so many different kinds of languages in the world, and none of those languages is without its own significance and distinction.

SN—Paul is still focusing here on his theme of clarity and understanding. He is now using the various languages of the world to, again, drive home this point. Though there are multitudes of languages all over the world, there is not one of them without its own linguistic significance, distinction, and therefore clear comprehension. Of all the languages in the world, there is not one of them that consists of unintelligible sounds. The very point of language is to clearly communicate a message to not only enable their understanding, but also to provide the opportunity for response.

14:11, BC—On the basis of what I just said, if I do not understand the meaning of a particular language, I will be like a foreigner with no ability to understand or communicate, and the one who is speaking to me will also be like a foreigner with no ability to understand or communicate.

SN—This theme of understanding is now stated by adding a new layer to the perspective. When I have no understanding of the language someone is speaking to me, there is an uncomfortable separation between us. Just as when you hear someone speaking a foreign language to you that you don't understand, you immediately feel uncomfortable and try to use some kind of motions or sign language to let them know you have no idea what they are saying. You feel as though there is an invisible wall between you. You know there is no point in continuing to hear these sounds that mean nothing to you. This same uneasy sense of being a foreigner is apparently an ongoing problem for the Corinthians with those who hear them.

14:12, BC—This message is for you, since you are so zealous and passionate to use the spiritual gifts. Make sure your use of them is always pointed toward the edification and building up of the church. Let edification be the focus of your passion to be the best.

SN—Now he takes the messages of all these illustrations and points them directly at the Corinthians. Paul is saying, "Don't use the gift as a self-centered exercise of passion but as a Body-centered exercise of sacrificial love. In your desire to be superior, be superior in nurturing love for the whole Body of Christ."

14:13, BC—On the basis of what I've said, let the one who speaks in a tongue also pray that he would be able to interpret.

SN—After the ongoing focus on interpretation and clarity of communication in the previous verses, Paul now approaches it in a different way. He now tries to show them their problem with the way they are using this gift. In these next few verses, he reveals the problematic issues. He chooses not to take the approach of demanding they stop using it but to dialogue with them in such a way that they will see why it doesn't work.

As we have seen previously, the Corinthians had fallen into a misuse of the gift of tongues. Perhaps partly because of the ecstatic utterance practiced in their pagan past and partly because of their immature obsession with the flashy, high-profile gift of tongues, they had become fixated on the spiritual excitement of ecstatic utterance. This became their spiritual experience of choice. They believed it was a spiritual gift, and they insisted on continuing to use it even though it was causing jealousy and division, brought no edification to the church, and caused Paul to write this scolding corrective. Paul is saying, "If you continue to insist on speaking in ecstatic utterance or unintelligible sounds, then you need to pray you could interpret and give clear communication and understanding to those hearing the sounds." Now, the problem to follow that directive becomes evident with this characterization of the prayer in the next verse.

14:14, BC—Because if I pray in a tongue, my spirit is praying in some kind of spiritual experience, but my understanding of what I am praying is fruitless, unproductive, and sterile.

SN—Now he makes the connection with the previous verse. If I pray in a tongue, which is an ecstatic utterance, my spirit prays and is enveloped in some kind of spiritual experience, but my understanding and mind are completely disengaged and have no comprehension of what I am praying. Paul is speaking of the Corinthian imitation of tongues with no understanding and comprehension involved, not the gift of tongues/languages as in Acts chapter 2 where there is understanding and comprehension.

Here is the crux of the problem. Not only does everyone around you have no understanding of the noise being produced, you also have no understanding of the noise being produced. Therefore, with absolutely no understanding or comprehension, there can be no interpretation and clear communication of a message. To have our minds and understanding completely disengaged and unproductive to what we are doing spiritually is not only pointless but actually even dangerous as is seen in the Corinthian experience.

14:15, BC—What is the conclusion, then, that I should come to concerning this? I will indeed pray with the spirit, and at the same time I will also pray with my understanding and comprehension. I will indeed sing with the spirit and in conjunction I will also sing with my understanding and comprehension.

SN—Paul now gives his resolution concerning this issue. He asks a question and then answers it. "What is my conclusion to be?" Paul asks. "Yes, I will be praying with my spirit, but instead of having my mind and understanding completely disengaged and unfruitful, as in your prayer, I will have them completely engaged and bearing fruit to the glory of God with every part of my being. Yes, I will be singing with my spirit, but instead of having my mind and understanding completely disengaged and unfruitful as in your song, I will have them completely engaged and bearing fruit to the glory of God with every part of my being. Paul is striving to share with them how they are short-circuiting the spiritual process.

14:16, BC—If you do not have both the spirit and the understanding involved together, if someone hears you uttering a blessing with only the spirit involved in some kind of ecstatic utterance or unintelligible sounds, how will someone who is uninformed about these utterances join you in saying "amen" to your giving of thanks, since he has no understanding or comprehension of what you are saying?

SN—Paul now uses a hypothetical scenario within the church to illustrate his point. In connecting to the previous verse, Paul is saying if you don't connect both the spirit and the understanding, this will short-circuit the spiritual edification process within the church family. If you are trying to bless the Lord or offer a prayer of thanksgiving with only the spirit involved through a tongue of ecstatic utterance or unintelligible sounds, you are robbing the others in the church body of any mutual edification. When one of them who is uninformed concerning these unintelligible sounds hears you speaking, it is impossible for them to join together with you in the blessing and give their confirmation. The real problem is they have no understanding or comprehension of what you're saying, and this makes it impossible to join in and be edified, which short-circuits God's purpose.

14:17, BC—For you are certainly striving to give thanks with passionate and sincere intent, but the other persons listening are not edified and built up in Christ.

SN—This is a conclusion to the previous verses. Paul as a pastor/shepherd is not castigating them with harsh discipline but rather is striving to counsel and guide. He is saying, "I acknowledge that you are striving to use this tongue of ecstatic utterance to give thanks to the Lord with passion and sincerity, but the serious problem for the church family and others still remains. God's design and intention in giving the spiritual gifts was to edify and build up the whole Body of Christ. Please understand that with your use of this gift, it is impossible to fulfill the design of God."

14:18, BC—I am thankful to my God that I have been used to speak with tongues/languages more than all of you.

SN—After addressing the shortcomings of the Corinthian use of tongues, Paul now speaks of his own experience. He seems to want them to know that while he is trying to give them correction concerning this gift, he is not denying the true gift itself. He certainly believes in and uses himself as an example of the genuine use of the spiritual gift. Even this personal testimonial will be followed by another corrective.

He gives thanks to God for giving him the spiritual gift of tongues/languages. God used Paul all over the known world in his mission journeys to speak the Word of God in known human languages, some of which he had never studied or learned, just as it was initiated in Acts chapter 2. This wonderful gift astonished the hearers, enabled them to hear clearly in their own language, and certainly authenticated the supernatural power of God as the source behind the new church and its messengers. Paul was one of God's main instruments to share the message in that beginning era of the church. Therefore, Paul was very familiar with this spiritual gift and had used it more than any of the Corinthians.

14:19, BC—But in the church I would much rather speak five words with my understanding and comprehension so I would then have the ability to teach others also, rather than to speak ten thousand words in a tongue as you do with no understanding.

SN—This is the completion of the sentence begun in the previous verse. Paul is making a specific point again about the spiritual gifts and their practice within the church body. Paul is saying, "When I am speaking in the church I want you to understand my position and priority in using the spiritual gifts."

He has gone to great lengths in the previous verses of this chapter to characterize their use of a tongue as a spiritual experience without any understanding attached. It was a spiritual experience that was self-centered and void of any understanding or comprehension and therefore fell short of God's design for edification and benefit of the whole Church. Now, for the sake of this argument and specific teaching point, he is employing a scenario using their own spiritual experience and practice to again highlight the priority of edification.

If he were to be speaking in some unknown tongue or ecstatic utterance in the church (which he has repeatedly castigated them for doing through these verses), he would far rather be able to speak just five words of it with understanding and comprehension so he could fulfill God's design by teaching and edifying others also, rather than to speak ten thousand words of it without any understanding or comprehension as they were currently doing. In other words, if it were possible to use the ecstatic utterance tongue and have some tiny fraction of it (1/2000th) understood, which could then produce edification, it would be far better than multi-thousands or an endless stream of meaningless words/sounds with no comprehension and no benefit to others in the Body of Christ.

God's Design Is for a Sign to Unbelievers

14:20, BC—Brothers and sisters in Christ, don't be spiritually immature like little children in your understanding of the spiritual gifts and their meanings; however, in the area of jealous anger and divisiveness toward one another be immature like innocent little babies. But concerning spiritual understanding be mature.

SN—Immediately on the heels of all the preceding correctives concerning their misuse and abuse of tongues, Paul now makes a plea for spiritual maturity. He is calling on them to grow up and become adults in their understanding and practice of the spiritual gift of tongues. He exhorts them not to be children any longer in the way they use spiritual gifts.

When my beautiful little three-year-old granddaughter comes to visit us, it is always an exciting event. She runs in the front door yelling Papa and Gigi, and we scoop her up in our arms and give her a big hug and kiss. We play games together and sometimes even see her climb up on the coffee table and begin to perform the latest song she has learned. With all the drama and body movements she can muster, she gives a performance that brings everything else in the house to a screeching halt. She is the center of attention and to her, at that moment, nothing else really matters. It just so happens that when she is on top of the coffee table with arms outstretched she is blocking my view of the TV (though I would really rather watch her). Though I may have been watching an important news report or more importantly in Oklahoma a severe weather warning concerning a tornado, it makes no difference to her because in her immaturity she has little concern about my needs or other important issues. As a spunky three-year-old, her concern is completely enveloped with her performance and her desires. The immaturity of a child is generally expressed in behavior that is self-centered and rarely others-centered, though I know my little sweetie will grow out of that stage and become a giving, mature adult.

This kind of self-centered immaturity is what Paul is addressing in the Corinthians' behavior and practice of spiritual gifts and especially of tongues. They have been like children with their own agenda to carry out and lacking in true love and compassion for the needs of others. This to a large degree had created the disunity he spoke of in chapter 12 and had revealed the lack of true love he spoke about in chapter 13. They had been too often focused on their own experience and negligent concerning the edification and needs of their brothers and sisters around them. Paul does call on them to be as immature and innocent as a newborn baby concerning any kind of jealous anger or divisiveness, but again calls on them to be mature in their spiritual understanding.

14:21, BC—In the Old Testament scripture, it is written, "with men of foreign tongues/languages and through their lips I will speak to this people of Israel, but even after this sign of judgment they still will not hear Me says the Lord" (paraphrase).

SN—Now Paul turns to the Old Testament scripture to reveal God's original reason for the gift of tongues/languages. The Jews were, and are, God's chosen people. They have a special place in God's plan and purpose, and He has continually tried to call them away from rejection and disobedience back to repentance and obedience. He is not finished with the nation of Israel.

In this Old Testament scripture out of Isaiah 28:11–12, Paul is referring back to a time in Israel's history when God was again trying to impact His chosen people and speak words of instruction through His prophet to cause them to repent and return to Him. Because they refused to hear the prophet's words and once again rejected God's call, He would bring judgment through foreign people with foreign languages. The Assyrians became God's rod of judgment, and as they spoke their foreign language to the captive Jews it was a sign that judgment had come. God used these men of other languages to speak to and provoke His people, and even after all that pain and judgment they still did not hear Him and obey.

This verse is crucially important to the understanding of Paul's teaching on the Corinthians' use of ecstatic utterance as a supposed spiritual gift of tongues. The tongues referred to in this Old Testament passage are unmistakably the known foreign languages of the nations whom God used to call the Jews to repentance, not some kind of unintelligible sounds. The Corinthians' use of ecstatic utterance would have no connection to the foreign languages God used for His purpose at that former time, or to the purposes that would follow.

With this use of Old Testament scripture and God's purpose for using foreign tongues/languages as a sign to the Jewish people, Paul also draws the parallel to the foreign languages/tongues used at Pentecost as another sign to the Jewish people. Dr. Zodhiates comments, "The apostle Paul quoted a prophecy from Isaiah 28:11 and 12 to prove that it was God's purpose to speak 'with men of other tongues' as a special witness to the Jews. Paul was drawing a parallel between the disobedience of the nations of Judah and the Northern Kingdom of Israel to God in Isaiah's day, and the disobedience of the Jews of Paul's day to God" (Zodhiates 1983, 126).

In Paul's day, the Jews had rejected God's call through the Messiah. "He came to His own, and His own did not receive Him" (John 1:11). God had used foreign languages at Pentecost, not only to share His Word and authenticate the message and messengers, but also as another sign of judgment to come to all the Jews dwelling in Jerusalem, "from every nation under heaven" (Acts 2:5). Not many years after Paul wrote this book, Jerusalem was completely destroyed in AD 70, fulfilling a sign of judgment to come.

The miraculous gift of foreign languages used at Pentecost was not for some kind of individual, spiritual catharsis for the one speaking but for God's call to the Jews and a sign of judgment to come without repentance.

14:22, BC—On the basis of what I just said, tongues/languages are meant as a sign, not to those who believe but to the unbelievers, but on the other hand prophesying is not for the unbelievers but for those who believe.

SN—Paul now follows up from the history lesson on tongues/languages from the previous verse. The miraculous gift of tongues/languages as God used them were as a sign. A sign is something that points to a specific purpose or in a specific direction. This sign, as God used it, was not for the purpose of declaring a specific message and teaching to the believers but for declaring a specific message and teaching to the unbelievers.

As this spiritual sign gift from God was used at Pentecost, not too many years previous to the Corinthian letter, its purpose was to supernaturally declare the message of God to the unbelievers there. This was obviously achieved, as they were astonished and knew that only God could produce such a miracle. It was both the call of God to repent and turn back to God through Christ and the sign of judgment to come and the accompanying consequences without repentance.

The Corinthians had pursued just the opposite of this intended purpose. They had begun to use the Corinthian tongue as a kind of spiritual exercise within the church. It had become a widely used gift within the fellowship of believers and further practiced by many of them all at the same time. Its use had also become directed toward the individual believer and his own personal cathartic experience. Paul tries to explain that this was misdirected, immature, and foreign to God's purpose.

Paul then gives the contrasting statement. "But prophesying is not for unbelievers but for those who believe." The gift of prophecy used to proclaim the truths of God's Word in how to love and serve Christ were obviously for believers. It was the dispensing of spiritual truth that would teach and enable believers to continue to learn and grow in their journey from salvation to the end of this life and even what was beyond in eternity. Paul continually tries to point the Corinthians back to this primary need instead of the cathartic spiritual exercises with which they were so heavily involved.

14:23, BC—On the basis of what I just said, if the whole body of believers comes together in one place and everyone begins to speak with tongues, and some people come in who are uninformed about these things or are even unbelievers who have no spiritual understanding at all, won't they say you are out of your mind?

SN—Paul now uses a hypothetical case to drive home his point concerning their practice. There seems to be a conflict between the previous verse and this one. Didn't Paul just explain to them that tongues were a sign for unbelievers? Didn't he just insist that this spiritual gift was actually pointed at unbelievers as is clearly seen in Acts chapter 2? How is it that now he states that the unbelievers coming into their meeting will have no understanding or comprehension of what is being spoken and think they have lost their mind? How is it that in the Corinthian fellowship this spiritual gift would have no convicting, redeeming quality for the unbelievers?

Not only is there no conflict between these verses, it is actually a confirmation of Paul's distinction between the tongues/languages of Acts chapter 2 and tongues as practiced by the Corinthians. At Pentecost, the unbelievers understood and comprehended the words of God spoken to them in known human languages through the miraculous means of the gift of tongues. At Corinth, in contrast to that, the unbelievers would come in and hear the multitude of ecstatic utterances and have no understanding or comprehension, which could only lead them to think that all the believers were hallucinating or out of their minds. This Corinthian imitation of tongues would not only fail to convey God's message to the unbelievers, but would also scare them away from their only hope in Christ. At Pentecost, the unbelievers didn't think the speakers were out of their minds. At Corinth, the unbelievers would think the speakers were out of their minds. At Pentecost, God spoke. At Corinth, the Corinthians spoke.

14:24, BC—But on the other hand if everyone was prophesying, proclaiming the truth of God's Word in the power of the Holy Spirit and an unbeliever or an uninformed person comes into your meeting, he will be convinced of the truth from God's Word that he hears you all speaking and he will be convicted by it.

SN—Paul proclaims the priority and power of prophesying. In the same scenario as in the previous verse, if the whole church came together and everyone began prophesying, then the outcome would be drastically different. If the unlearned or unbelievers came into the meeting and heard the believers proclaiming the truths of God's Word in their own language, then the Holy Spirit would begin to work in their lives. From the truths of God's Word planted in their hearts, they would be convinced by the living truth and convicted of their sin and need to turn to Christ. The Holy Spirit would use these convicting truths as a spiritual mirror of sorts to facilitate an internal examination.

At first glance, it may seem odd that in verse 22 Paul states that prophesying is not for unbelievers but for those who believe, and now in this verse he speaks of the wonderful benefit to the unbeliever. First, he is making a statement of contrast in verse 22 and is not dictating a literal absolute, as we know that God's Word is living and powerful and able to touch any life. Second, the whole of scripture is a treasure book of unlimited learning and growing for the believer over a lifetime, and prophecy is primarily pointed in that direction. However, while prophecy is primarily pointed toward the believer, there is also the convicting work of God's truth that draws an unbeliever to repentance and faith in Christ.

14:25, BC—And because of that convicting work of the Holy Spirit through God's Word, the inner secrets of his heart are revealed. He then falls down on his face in humility and repentance and begins to worship God and confesses that God is truly in your midst.

SN—This is the wonderful result of hearing the truths of God's Word proclaimed and the work of the Holy Spirit in applying those truths to a person's heart. When the bright light of God's convicting truth trains its spotlight on the dark innermost secrets of the heart, the shocking reality of our bondage is revealed. When we truly see our sin and fully realize it was laid upon the battered and bloody body of our Lord Jesus Christ on the cross, our hearts can only find one response. In deep humility and repentance, we fall down on our faces before such sacrificial love. We begin to worship this Almighty, forgiving God and begin to tell everyone that He is truly in this place and evident in the lives of these believers. Spiritual transformation takes place.

Paul's contrast between the Corinthians' use of tongues and the spiritual gift of prophecy couldn't be any clearer. When unbelievers hear the Corinthians' imitation of tongues, they will be confused. When unbelievers hear the spiritual gift of prophecy, they will be convicted. When unbelievers hear the Corinthians' imitation of tongues, there will be no understanding and comprehension. When unbelievers hear the spiritual gift of prophecy, there will be revealing understanding and comprehension. When unbelievers hear the Corinthians' imitation of tongues, they will be repulsed by the seeming madness. When unbelievers hear the spiritual gift of prophecy, they will be compelled by truth. When unbelievers hear the Corinthians' imitation of tongues, they will leave with even more questions than they had before. When unbelievers hear the spiritual gift of prophecy, they will leave transformed with many of life's deepest questions answered.

God's Design Is for Purpose and Order

14:26, BC—So why is it, my brothers and sisters in Christ, that whenever you come together that every one of you has a Psalm to speak, a teaching to explain, a tongue to use, a revelation to reveal, or an interpretation to give? Let everything you do be done for edification of the whole Body.

SN—Paul presses further with the shortsightedness of their ministry. Their gatherings seem to be focused on all of them as individuals. They were all striving to do their own thing. Their coming together as a Body was short-circuited because they all came with their own spiritual agenda. They couldn't minister to and edify one another because they were all functioning within their own spiritual bubble.

As the corrective in some of the following verses will reveal, they were not only acting individually, but they were acting individually all at the same time. There was spiritual chaos as they were all supposedly exercising their own gifts simultaneously. One sang a Psalm, while another tried to explain truth, while another spoke in a tongue, while another spoke a revelation, while still another gave an interpretation. Whatever legitimacy and truth there was within this mixture, it was drowned out because no one else was hearing. They were all intent on divulging their own message simultaneously. This tongue seemed to be the Corinthian imitation, as it was self-centered in its orientation (everyone speaking at the same time and functioning within their own spiritual bubble) and totally devoid of any kind of edification for the whole Body of Christ.

This was certainly not God's design for spiritual gifts. Paul again tries to correct this mentality and drag them back to the divine focus. There was to be one overriding principle in all they did as a church family. Whether singing, teaching, speaking in a tongue, sharing a revelation, or interpretation, it was all to be done with a focus on edification and building up the whole Body of Christ. This was not a suggestion and it was not optional. In order to fulfill God's purpose within the Body of Christ, everything must have the goal of edification, not selfication.

14:27, BC—When you come together, if anyone is going to speak in a tongue, let it be just two of you or at the very most three. Let each one speak one at a time and when they are done the next one can take his turn. Also, make sure that one interprets everything spoken.

SN—Paul takes a practical approach to address the problem in the previous verse. He gives specific guidelines to avert the chaos of simultaneous chatter. If someone is going to speak in a tongue when they come together, the preference is to limit it to only two people but never more than three. This was a drastic difference from the simultaneous free-for-all he addressed earlier with many people involved. The limitation was then pressed further as these two or three were never supposed to be speaking simultaneously, but one at a time. The final condition in this verse is that each one of them must have an interpretation.

Paul's effort to corral this Corinthian tongue is clearly seen. Before it had been completely out of control and chaotic. There had been numerous people all speaking in unintelligible sounds, and all of those sounds had been garbled together simultaneously. With everyone speaking at the same time, it was also obvious that any attempted interpretations were part of the mass mix. The result was no understanding, which meant no clear message, which meant no edification, which meant a failure to follow God's design.

At least these guidelines would cut down on the chaos and confusion. Rather than the previous free-for-all, one person would get up and speak by himself. After he was done speaking, an interpreter would get up and speak whatever interpretation he had. After that, the second person would get up and do the same, followed by an interpretation. Sometimes a third might follow suit. After that, it was done. There would be no more randomly jumping up and speaking in a tongue. There would be no more simultaneous chaos. It had, in a sense, been put in its place.

It is interesting to note the apparent effectiveness with which Paul curtailed the Corinthians' use of a tongue. It is never mentioned again in his second letter to this same church family or for that matter in any of the other letters he wrote. Knowing Paul's courage and determination, he certainly would not have been hesitant to deal with it in the second letter if it had been an ongoing problem.

14:28, BC—But if there is not an interpreter present, the one who is going to speak in a tongue should keep silent in the church meeting. He should only speak to himself and to God.

SN—Paul is reinforcing the requirements just given. In light of the previous chaotic behavior in their church meetings, he effectively brings a complete end to the random, impulsive use of a tongue without an interpreter. Though someone may have a passionate desire to speak in a tongue during the worship service, if there is not an interpreter present in the same service, it is forbidden.

The overall effect of Paul's instructions concerning speaking in a tongue is now coming into full view. He is escorting them from a place of immaturity manifested by selfishness, jealousy, impulsiveness, and chaos to a place of maturity manifested by selflessness, understanding, thoughtfulness, and order. He is guiding them from their current practice of doing things with indecency and disorder to a place that honors God and His design by doing them decently and in order.

His final instruction in this verse to the one who has been prohibited from speaking in a tongue is to just speak silently to himself and to God. Dr. Patterson explains the use of the word *silent* in this verse. "The absence of an interpreter means that one who would speak must remain 'silent' (*sigato*), a strong word which calls for absolute silence"

(Patterson 1983, 262). Whatever the speaker wanted to say had to be redirected toward an internal dialogue between himself and God.

Dr. Patterson also discusses an interesting point concerning how this process was actually carried out. If the person wanting to speak in a tongue was required to have an interpreter before speaking, which is clear from this verse, then he or the leaders of the church must find an interpreter beforehand. Either they would have to know an interpreter was coming before the service or when the speaker had an urge to speak they would have to immediately find one in the service at that moment. Though we don't know exactly how they carried out that task, we can see some of the effect of Paul's directive. This action would radically curtail the immature and impulsive behavior that had dominated their church services and, in many cases, eliminate it altogether.

14:29, BC—Let two or three prophets speak their message and let the others examine that message.

SN—After dealing with the ones who wanted to speak in a tongue during the church service, Paul moves on to the ones with the gift of prophecy. He encourages two or three of the members with the gift of prophecy to use their gift to proclaim the truths of God's Word. This was the gift that Paul had repetitiously called attention to. Over and over again he had exhorted them to prioritize this gift in the assembly of believers and not the gift of tongues. He had held it up as an effective example of the edification of believers and in verses 24 and 25 had even touted its tremendous impact in the lives of unbelievers. In effect, Paul had said, "Do this and not that."

The second part of the verse speaks about the gift of prophecy being judged. Paul's strong caution about making sure that the words spoken were the true words of God, especially at this point before the completion of the New Testament, is even applied to this spiritual gift. Others with the spiritual gift of prophecy were to listen to those who were speaking and examine it. The Amplified version says, "So, let two or three prophets speak—those inspired to preach or teach—while the rest pay attention and weigh and discern what is said" (1 Corinthians 14:29, Amp.). As we have already seen, discernment is one of the spiritual gifts God gave to the Church. Even while exercising this gift of prophecy in the common language of the people, there was still spiritual accountability in place. With the supreme importance of an eternal life and death message at stake, the discernment of accurate truth was crucial.

With this principle in mind, it is even easier to see why there was a fearful problem with speaking in an unintelligible language that no one understood and for which there was no spiritual accountability.

14:30, BC—But if anything spiritually urgent is revealed to another with the gift of prophecy who is sitting there by him, let the first speaker stop and defer to him.

SN—Here we begin to see some of the selflessness and true love Paul had spoken of earlier. Though the gift of prophecy was prioritized by Paul as one of the most important spiritual gifts, the manner in which those gifts were used was also a priority. This kind of action would reveal not only the selflessness of a heart whose highest priority was to hear God's message, but also the grace to defer to another brother. This demonstrated a true brotherhood in Christ that could work together seamlessly in proclaiming the truth of God's Word as He gave direction by His Holy Spirit. Once again, we can't help but see this truth in light of the context of this chapter. Functioning within God's design, as we see here, there was accountability, humility, and gracious submission in contrast to the lack of accountability, humility, and gracious submission that was evidenced in the Corinthians' free-for-all.

14:31, BC—For you can all prophesy, proclaiming the truths of God's Word one at a time so that everyone may learn and everyone may be encouraged.

SN—Notice that Paul still retains the requirement of speaking one at a time, even with the gift of prophecy. The confusion and chaos of simultaneously speaking was eliminated with this directive. The very purpose for hearing the truths of God's Word proclaimed was to be able to clearly hear, process, and learn from those truths and to be encouraged by them. Without clearly hearing the proclamation, as in the Corinthians' meetings, the whole process was aborted and degenerated into some kind of synchronous experience of many sounds dissipating out into the air like a vapor.

14:32, BC—And the spirits of those who are prophesying are subject to and under the control of those who are prophesying.

SN—Paul is again drawing a contrast to the previous behavior of the Corinthians. The beautiful picture of order and accountability seen in verse 29, of selfless deference seen in verse 30, and of mutual learning and encouragement seen in verse 31 are the pictures of God's design. The marred picture of no order or accountability, no selfless deference, and no mutual learning and encouragement are the pictures of the Corinthians' meetings.

Those who use the gift of prophecy according to God's design have the control and ability of their own spirits—out of submission to the Holy Spirit's control in their lives—to choose to speak one at a time, to choose to be accountable to each other, to choose to be quiet in selfless deference to another, and to choose to be mutual learners and encouragers. The Corinthians' own spirits were, many times, not subject to them. As we have seen previously, they would impulsively burst into speaking in unintelligible noises with their minds and understanding completely detached from the experience. They would enter into some kind of rapturous spiritual experience where there was no control and no ability to choose to speak one at a time, to choose to be accountable to each other, to choose to be quiet in selfless deference to one another, or to choose to be mutual learners and encouragers. This was the out-of-control environment and mentality Paul tried to correct.

14:33, BC—For God is not the author and initiator of confusion and chaos but of peace as in all churches of the saints.

SN—There had been a great deal of confusion and chaos in the fellowship at Corinth. Everything ranging from everyone speaking at the same time to some of the members impulsively blurting out unintelligible sounds in an uncontrolled, mentally detached manner had run rampant in their services. They were all rapturously involved in their own spiritual pursuit in their own spiritual bubble. The environment had degenerated into something confusing and chaotic. Paul is giving them a look in the spiritual mirror at the source of the confusion and chaos. He wants them to see that the source was clearly not God. God has no confusion or disorder in Himself. He did not initiate nor does He condone confusion, especially in the Body of Christ. God has designed the Body of Christ to operate in peace and to pursue Him through heartfelt worship and praise. He has given His Word to the Church to be clearly communicated to produce edification. In his final letter to his son in Christ, Timothy, Paul wrote, "All Scripture is given by inspiration of God, and is profitable for doctrine, for reproof, for correction, for instruction in righteousness, that the man of God may be complete, thoroughly equipped for every good work" (2 Timothy 3:16–17). The profitable aspects of scripture had largely been missing in the confusion.

14:34, BC—Let your women keep silent on this matter in the churches because they do not have permission to speak in this way. Their habit of life is to be submissive as we see stated in the Old Testament scriptures.

SN—Several items need to be addressed to have a clearer understanding of what Paul is speaking to the women of the Corinthian Church. We need to see the related scriptures, the context, and the specific problem.

First, we need to be aware of some related scriptures to shed more light on the subject. To see this statement as completely forbidding women to ever utter a word in the church is to misunderstand Paul's statement. This position is also contradicted by related scripture. Dr. Patterson explains, "If Paul was saying that women are never to speak in the church, then he seems to have been in contradiction with himself when he allowed a woman to pray or prophesy provided her head was covered (11:5). In addition, there are other explicit references to women in teaching roles in the epistles of Paul" (Patterson 1983, 265).

Second, we need to pay careful attention to the context of this passage. To divorce this statement from the context of this passage is to see one piece of the puzzle without its whole. The unmistakable, larger context of this passage is Paul's correction concerning the misuse and abuse of spiritual gifts and especially the gift of tongues. Also, the immediate context of the verses just previous to this one concern the gift of prophecy and the examining of that gift by others in verse 29.

Third, we should also remember the specific problem with which Paul was dealing. He was dealing with the chaos and confusion of a spiritual free-for-all. There was widespread misuse and abuse of the gift of tongues which, of course, included women. In contradiction to God's pattern within the family of the wife's submissive attitude toward her husband, it seems the women were also launching out in their own independent spiritual pursuits. Leaving the protective connection with their husband, they were also being carried away by the rapturous spiritual ecstasy running uncontrolled through the congregation.

The context of the chapter clearly deals with the issue of speaking in tongues while the immediate context in the previous verses deals with the gift of prophecy and the examination of that gift. With all of the destructive behaviors going on in the church, Paul was trying to bring correction and restore God's design. Whether Paul was saying to the church that the women were not supposed to speak in tongues only or whether he included that it was not their place to examine and/or challenge the messages of prophecy is not completely clear. However, it was clear that they were not allowed to impulsively launch into ecstatic utterances with no appropriate regard for their husbands.

14:35, BC—If the women of the church want to learn more about spiritual things, let them ask questions and discuss the issues with their own husband at home because it is shameful for women to speak out in the church in this manner.

SN—The theme of God's designed order for the church and the family is continued. If it was the desire of the women to truly grow in Christ and learn more about spiritual things, it was not to be carried out in an open and possibly even confrontational manner in the church service. Though we don't have any exact details of the problems as they manifested themselves, judging from these strong words from the apostle, it seems likely that some women were in fact the source of some of the problems. Dr. Patterson comments, "Perhaps the women in the church at Corinth were not only the principle abusers of this gift of tongues but were also blatant in their questioning of those who stood to prophesy or to teach" (Patterson 1983, 266).

Whatever the details of the problems were in the divisive chaos at Corinth, it is clear from these words that some women were part of the problem. If their desire was to grow in Christ and learn more about spiritual things and the truths of God's Word that were presented, they were to ask their questions and even offer their challenges in the home environment with their husbands. God's design for the family was to have the father as the spiritual leader of the home to teach and clarify the truths presented from God's Word. For the wife to intentionally step away from God's design and independently and openly begin to speak in ecstatic utterance and/or question and challenge the truths being shared was rebellious and it was shameful.

14:36, BC—Or do you think that the Word of God came originally from you? Or are you the only ones who received it?

SN—For those in the Corinthian Church who were in spiritual rebellion and would pridefully reject Paul's counsel, he asks these questions with challenging sarcasm. He knew that those he had addressed, especially those claiming to be leaders in the area of prophecy and tongues and also the women, would bristle at his instructions. They would, of course, claim to know God's truth and insist they were following it. With the spiritual pride and arrogance that had been manifested and that he knew would again be manifested at the reception of this letter, he asks pointed questions. "Do you now think that the truths of the Word of God proclaimed there in Corinth originated from you? Do you think you are the only ones who received the truth and you are the chosen ones?"

In fact, they were not the ones who had originally shared the gospel of Christ, and they were not the only ones to have received the truth. Paul asks the questions with the intention of pointing them back to their gospel roots. Paul himself had actually been God's instrument in founding the church at Corinth and proclaiming God's Word to them. They were not the select few to whom the truth had come and who were now the leaders and purveyors of that truth. God had placed Paul in their lives as their founding pastor and spiritual father. That was their spiritual heritage and Paul was reminding them of it.

14:37, BC—If any one of you believes he is a prophet or a spiritual leader, let him acknowledge and confirm that the truths which I have written to you are the commandments of the Lord.

SN—This is, of course, another challenge to the leadership of the church. If you are spiritual leaders in the church who have true discernment from the Holy Spirit of God rather than an immature pride and arrogance, then prove it. I have shared with you the truths that God has given me through the inspiration and power of the Holy Spirit. If you are the spiritual leaders you say you are, then confirm to the members of the church at Corinth that the Holy Spirit-inspired truths I have sent to you in this letter are the commandments of the Lord. This was their test from Paul. It was also an incredibly bold statement from the apostle that what he had written to them was in fact God's Word. We don't know exactly how all the leaders responded to Paul's bold challenge. Some of them may have become angry, and some of them may have even separated themselves to create their own church. What we do know is that this spiritual battleground concerning the misuse and abuse of spiritual gifts, and especially tongues, was not visited again in the second letter to the Corinthians.

14:38, BC—But if anyone insists on being ignorant, then let him continue on in his ignorance.

SN—Anticipating the likely response from some of them, Paul instructs the others on how to deal with those who arrogantly refuse the instruction of God's Word directly from His apostle. If they choose to be spiritually ignorant and continue in the destructive chaos and confusion, then they will remain ignorant. The admonition was to let him continue in his ignorance, which would have to include not continuing to follow him in his ignorance. With the connection of these two verses, it seems obvious that Paul is instructing them not to follow a person such as this. His spiritual ignorance shown by his rejection of God's truths would disqualify him from spiritual leadership in the church.

14:39, BC—On the basis of my previous statements, my brothers and sisters in Christ, continue on with a strong desire to prophesy and proclaim the truths of God's Word and also don't forbid someone from speaking in tongues/languages.

SN—He now summarizes the theme of the chapter with the word *therefore*, which is just a way of saying, "on the basis of" or "with the understanding of the previous information." Paul returns in the final analysis to his priority of prophecy, which was proclaiming the truths of God's Word. The Corinthian Church needed to prioritize the use of prophecy instead of the obsessive use of tongues. He says earnestly desire, covet, or run after the gift that brings edification, encouragement, and conviction rather than the gift that had engendered confusion and chaos.

After his final attempt to permanently tattoo on their hearts the vital importance and priority of prophecy, he shares a conciliatory word on tongues/languages. In those beginning years of the new church era, Paul still left the door open for the possibility of God using the gift of tongues/languages as in Acts chapter 2. With all of the restrictions and prohibitions put in place to eliminate chaos and confusion, Paul left a legitimate door open for the genuine gift in that transitional period.

14:40, BC—Let everything that you do in the church be done decently, in a way worthy of our Lord's worship, and in order, with an appropriate decorum.

SN—Now, in conclusion after three chapters of correctives, Paul states his final principle. His exhortation concerns every part of the corporate services. In everything you do in the church, let this be your guiding principle. Let it be done decently and in order. Worship the Lord and use the spiritual gifts He has given to the Church decently, in a way that is worthy of the King of kings and Lord of lords. Also, make sure they are used with the appropriate beauty and order that would honor the indescribable God Whom we worship.

That's His Love

The secret sin you hid so well,
that trapped you in your private hell
Was laid on Him, the price He paid
to free you from the choice you made

That's His love, the Savior's love

The guilt and shame that clouds your soul,
that hopeless hurt that took its toll
When no one's there, when no one hears,
He knows your heart, He feels your tears

That's His love, the Savior's love

The road seems long, the problems great,
the questions hard, the answers late
Take heart, dear child, for you He came
to beat all sin, all hell, and shame

That's His love, the Savior's love

No sin too great, no fall too far,
His arm can reach to where you are
You cannot run beyond His love,
He sees each step from heaven above

That's His love, the Savior's love.

January 2008

Part 3: My Gifts

Chapter 8
The Big Search

Searching for My Gifts

After graduation from Penney High School in Hamilton, Missouri, in 1972, I moved with my family to Fort Collins, Colorado, the home of Colorado State University (CSU). My dad began to pastor in the little town of Bellevue just outside Fort Collins. He also became a pastoral advisor to the Baptist Student Union (BSU) on campus at CSU. Though I was not going to college there, I began to attend the BSU meetings. I met some great Christian young people there, along with Robert the director, and began to enjoy the fellowship. One of the young ladies who actually lived at the BSU house was Gretchen. We began to date and fall in love, and on July 13, 1973, we were married.

Gretchen had committed her life to Jesus Christ before I arrived, due to the love and ministry of those BSU students. They had invited her to a revival at one of the local churches, and it was there she had committed her life to Christ. When we met, I, of course, told her I was a Christian and had always carried that label. However, the truth was I only had the label. I had tried to live as I thought a Christian should live and act like I thought a Christian should act (doing a terrible job of it) while still unchanged on the inside. Not long after we were married, I realized something was terribly wrong in my life. I wept and prayed for several days searching for answers. I finally realized that though I had called myself a Christian, I had never been changed on the inside. That was a defining moment as I wept alone in the church office that day, and I surrendered everything to Jesus Christ.

Change on the Inside

After I truly surrendered my heart and life to Jesus Christ as my personal Lord and Savior, I could tell I was different on the inside. I had lived for many years trying to act like a Christian and after this drastic change, I knew that that was exactly what it had been, an act. Now it was no longer an act. Now it was life change from the inside. Before, it had all been external and performance based. Now I noticed that my internal desires and motives had changed. Before, my attempt to live as a Christian was basically works oriented and therefore carried out as a burdensome duty. Now I realized it was all grace and that Christ was actually living out His life through me, and it was empowering.

Not long after my salvation, I began to feel a desire in my heart to serve in ministry. I knew this was evidence of a serious change in my heart, as I had grown up watching my father pastoring with a slew of heartaches and problems. As I had watched him being attacked, not only by the world but by the very people within our church, it truly saddened me and, if I'm being honest, made me very angry. Growing up, I watched this play out time after time in church after church. It seemed to be one difficulty after another and one move after another. Through my elementary and high-school years, I had made eight school moves.

Even with this past track record of pain and anger, things were now different. Since becoming a new creature in Christ, there was a fire lit in my heart and it was growing. Now the pain and anger had been replaced by love and passion. I no longer wanted to serve out of burdensome duty; I was filled with love for Jesus and a desire to serve Him. I was young and passionate but still allowing the flesh to control too many areas of my life. Though I was still growing and struggling through some of those fleshly desires, the passion in my heart pushed me forward.

A New Chapter

A year or two after my salvation, my desire to serve the Lord in vocational ministry became evident to everyone. On March 2, 1975, I was licensed to preach the gospel of Jesus Christ at Bellevue Baptist Church in Bellevue, Colorado, where my dad was pastor. This was another defining moment in my life, as I knew my path had changed forever.

At that time in my life, the fire in my heart to serve Jesus in ministry only continued to grow. I also had a love in my heart for music, so I began to be involved in music ministry. For the next several years, as I worked in construction, I was also growing and ministering through music. I bought a sound system and some tapes and began to sing and lead music in revivals at every opportunity.

In those beginning years, I really didn't have a concept of spiritual gifts. I just knew the Lord had called me into ministry, and I was diving in to follow that call. I had heard the term "spiritual gifts" and had probably even listened to my dad preach messages numerous times on the subject. At that point in my life and ministry, they were simply words. I assumed that whatever I needed Jesus had given me, and I continued to move forward.

I'm certainly not recommending this approach to young people who are preparing for or in ministry. It would have been great to have a mentor teach me about the spiritual gifts from scripture and help me be fully aware of what God had placed in my life to effectively serve Him. That was just not my experience. In my search, I just began to study God's Word and learn pieces here and there. As I shared in more detail in the beginning chapters of this book, I was told many things by many people concerning spiritual gifts in those early years. Some of it was in line with some of the Bible studies I had attended, but some of it was radically different, especially concerning the gift of tongues and being baptized in the Holy Spirit. That brought me to another defining moment in my life and my journey of intense study and prayer that I have outlined in the earlier chapters of this book. The big search through spiritual gifts began.

Now after looking back at over forty years of walking with the Lord and studying His precious Word, things are much clearer. I've studied the original language along with a host of other books on the subject. Like many of you, I have taken spiritual gifts assessment surveys numerous times to help determine and/or confirm the grace gifts in my life.

It became evident to me early on in my studies that God had placed several spiritual gifts in my life. After some years in ministry, I believed God had called me as a pastor and gifted me in that area along with administration and even helps. The gift of "teachers" mentioned in 1 Corinthians 12 most likely corresponds to the pastor-teacher category of Ephesians 4:11. This gift is used to effectively explain the truths of God's Word and make application to the lives of those in the church.

The gift of "administrations" is also translated "governments" and is found in the same passage. This word originally had to do with the helmsman guiding a ship safely through its passage. It came to mean one who could give clear counsel and direction in spiritual matters. The gift of "helps," which is also recorded in the same passage, speaks of the ability to see those in serious need and in some sense become a burden bearer with them.

A New Realization

While I was familiar with these gifts for many years and watched how God used them in my life in different situations, I confess that with hindsight I am also realizing something else God has used in my life. I am hesitant to even mention it as a possible gift in my life because of my flaws and shortcomings, and many times not living up to it, but it is the gift of "faith," and I want to honor the Lord with everything He has done in my life. In reference to this gift in 1 Corinthians 12:9, Dr. Lowery writes, "Faith as a spiritual gift is probably an unusual measure of trust in God beyond that exercised by most Christians" (Walvoord and Zuck 1983, 533).

By that definition, it is possible that most all of us could believe God has used it in our lives at one time or another. Whether or not it is a gift in my life some may question, but I am sure as I look back that God has filled me with a desire and trust in Him that was beyond me. That fact became even more apparent as I began to write some of these testimonies in my life and view them not as separate events but as an incredible collage running through my whole life. Even now after all these years, I am seeing this new theme running through my life that was not fully apparent to me as I was actually living through those events. Maybe it will be some help and encouragement to you to see how God worked through these experiences. Perhaps you will see yourself and your gifts more clearly or perhaps God will open your eyes as He has mine and reveal something you hadn't seen before. I pray that will be the case and that you will be blessed as I share some of these interventions of God in my life.

He's Jesus the Lord

For thirty-three years He lived this life,
with family and friends, with critics and strife
From outward appearance His life missed the mark,
no riches, no home, the end very dark

With three awful nails they hung Him there,
a criminal's death, what pain and despair
From outward appearance His death was for naught,
they mocked and they yelled, triumphant they thought.

For three darkened days, they left Him there,
His body entombed and guarded with care
From outward appearance His tomb was the end,
a life that was gone, no more hearts to mend

Thirty-three years, three nails and three days,
from cradle to cross to borrowed grave
The span of a life that had slipped away,
thirty-three years, three nails and three days

But early on Sunday morning they came,
expecting to find His body the same
His body was gone and true to His claim,
He rose up again His power to proclaim

He's Jesus the Lord, the King of all kings
He's Jesus the Lord, to Him I will sing
Creator, Almighty, He sits on the throne
He's Jesus the Lord, He rolled back the stone.

May 2007

Chapter 9
The Big Leap

Move It!

Just a few years after God called me into ministry, I remember one of our first faith-building experiences. We were living in a small trailer in Fort Collins, Colorado. After doing music ministry in revivals for a few years, God had opened the door for my first official, part-time ministry position at a church in town. I was called as a music and youth worker and was thrilled to begin. I began planning and leading the music on Sundays and also working with the youth. In my youthful enthusiasm, I tried all kinds of things with the youth to connect with them and make it more exciting. Some of my ideas were good and some not so good. I remember at one youth event I had decided it would be really fun to have a challenge game like dodgeball, only instead of dodgeball, I decided to make it more interesting and use eggs and tomatoes. We all went outside, lined up, and on my signal started the free-for-all. You can probably imagine the outcome with teenagers throwing eggs and tomatoes at each other. Needless to say, the parents were not too happy with me after seeing the welts on their kids. I never did it again.

After I had been at the church for a short time, the pastor resigned. While the church began its search for a new full-time pastor, they asked me to consider filling in as the interim pastor. Though I was young with no experience, I was excited to be asked and told them I would accept the position. With the same enthusiasm I had poured into the youth ministry, I began to study and prepare messages to try and be the best leader I knew how to be.

Every facet of being a pastor was a new experience for me. Some of those experiences went well, and some of them not so well. I remember being very excited about my first opportunity to baptize a young lady after she gave her heart to Christ. I scheduled her baptism on a beautiful, but very cold Colorado Sunday morning in January. I arrived at the church very early that morning to run the water in the baptistery and turn the heater on. I then went to the study and began to look over my message for that morning and spend some time in prayer. Afterward, I came back to the baptistery to check and make sure everything was ready. To my shock, when I stuck my hand in the water it felt like mountain water out of the river. I hadn't realized that the heater had to be left on overnight for around fourteen hours to heat the water. It had been on for just over an hour, and this water was still so cold it would take your breath away.

When she arrived that morning, I told her what had happened and having invited her whole family to be there she decided to take the plunge. As she walked down the steps into the baptistery that morning, she gasped like we had just broken the ice on a pond and were wading in. She stood in the water by me shivering as I said the words I heard my father say many times before. I felt bad enough about the cold water, but there was one other thing I had forgotten to do. I didn't wipe out the baptistery ahead of time. That may not sound like a big problem to you, but as I lowered her down into the water, it became a big problem for me. There was a big bug the size of my thumbnail floating around in the water. As I put her under the water, the movement of the water brought the bug immediately over her face. My thought was, *I can't panic and ruin the (cold) beauty of this young lady's sacred moment.* As I pushed her sideways and brought her back up out of the water, the bug was on her white robe. I brushed it off and tried to look as normal as possible. Not my finest hour.

With all these new experiences, my heart began to be burdened about Bible college. I was doing my best, but knew I needed training to move forward and more effectively serve the Lord. My dad had completed a doctor of ministry degree at Luther Rice Seminary in Jacksonville, Florida, and I began to inquire about the school. I got more information and began to pray about this possibility. After praying about it, I felt sure the Lord wanted me to begin my training there. This became one of those faith-building, defining moments in our lives. I knew we were supposed to go, but we didn't have the money to go. It was one of those first moments when you have to decide that you're going to either trust God and walk by faith against all the odds and even against the advice of good people, or let fear make the decision and stay. Some probably believed it was foolish and crazy, and I certainly don't recommend it to anybody else, but I knew God was calling and I had to go. We loaded up what few things we had in a U-Haul trailer, put our two little ones in the car, and headed for Florida. I believe God wanted to see if we would trust Him even when we didn't see how it would work. We pulled away from that little trailer that day without even enough money for gas to make it to Florida. Was it bold faith or foolish immaturity? You can make your own judgment. What happened? God was faithful as He always is. He provided through somebody we saw while on the trip, and we made it to our destination. I don't know if that meets our definition of, "an unusual measure of trust in God beyond that exercised by most Christians," but it was a huge faith-building step for us.

Mail It!

Another one of those faith-building moments came a couple years later when I was attending Luther Rice Bible College. Obviously, our move out to Jacksonville had been a financial struggle. I was trying to go to school full time, lead a youth ministry part time, and work part time at the school as a handyman. It was a walk of faith and money was very tight. In the course of a semester or two, we had fallen way behind on our bills.

One Sunday, the pastor at our little church in Jacksonville had given me the opportunity to preach. That Sunday morning I preached a message on faith. Little did I know at the time that God would turn the message around and point its finger in my face. As we were driving home from church that Sunday, I was under great conviction. I shared with Gretchen in the car that if I was going to preach about faith, we needed to be the example of living by faith. That set in motion what came next.

Please understand as I share this experience that I am not recommending my actions to anyone else, but this was a work of faith building that God was doing in my life and I knew it. We had fallen so far behind in our finances that we had over $900 in overdue bills. At that time in our lives, that was an impossible amount to us. I made $75 to $100 every two weeks as a handyman and a small amount from church as part-time youth minister. There was no way to catch up.

This was another one of those defining moments when I felt like I was supposed to step out in faith and do something radical. I gathered all the bills together and desperately prayed that God would meet these needs. I then wrote out checks for over $900 of bills. The checking account was near empty before I wrote the checks. I thought to myself, *Either God will honor this step of faith or I will probably go to jail in a few days.* I put them in the envelopes, put the stamps on them, and headed for the mailbox. It was a struggle as I walked up to put them in the mailbox. The thoughts were running through my mind. *Is this really faith or is this stupidity? Is this really an act of faith or is it just desperation?* I know what you're probably thinking and, believe me, I understand. However, I stuck the bills in the mail.

As Gretchen and I prayed over these bills, we prayed God would provide for all of these bills plus about $160 for a plane ticket for her to go visit her parents in Pennsylvania. I could hardly wait to go and get our mail the next day. I thought surely the Lord would send something through someone in the mail after my bold step of faith. There was nothing! I was a little discouraged but decided I would wait in faith. The next day I went to get the mail and was expecting a surprise. There was nothing. Things were now getting very serious, and I began to question myself knowing the third or fourth day I was in trouble.

I went to my evening class at Bible college with a heavy heart. I didn't want to be there, but I went anyway. Sometimes we would begin our classes with someone sharing a testimony about something God had done in his or her life. That particular night one of my friends, who was a street preacher in the city, got up to share. He had scraped together enough money to build a little plywood trailer he pulled behind his car. He would pull the trailer around the city and stop on a busy street, get up on top of the trailer, and begin to share the gospel of Christ with whoever was passing by. He didn't have much money and what he did have he used for his ministry. Over three decades have passed since that night, and I sit here with tears in my eyes remembering it like it was yesterday.

He told us that the last few days while he was praying God kept laying Brother Mark on his heart. I hadn't talked to him, and he knew nothing of my financial situation other than the fact that all of us students were poor. He said for several months he had been saving his change and any other money he could in order to buy some new equipment for his preaching trailer. Then came one of the great shocks of my life as I sat there thinking I had probably done something stupid and would soon pay a price. He told all of us in the class that God told him to give all that money he had been saving to Brother Mark. He went on to tell us that his response to God was that he had saved that money specifically for his ministry and didn't want to give it all away. He said God told him again the second time to give all that money he had saved to Brother Mark. Again, he balked in his response. God spoke again and he lovingly submitted. He walked over to my chair and handed me a tattered, plastic bread sack full of change and some bills. I was overwhelmed with emotion and simply hugged him and thanked him. Somebody tapped my shoulder from behind me, and I turned around to be handed another check from one of my other brother students in the class. I was at church the next day, and the organist handed me another personal check. When I went home I sat down and figured out the money we had been given so I could deposit it in the bank before the cops came to get me. The total amount of money given to us paid over $900 of bills and guess how much was left. Yes, it was $160. Was this an "unusual measure of trust in God beyond that exercised by most Christians"? I don't know. Was it faith or just crazy? All I know is if it was crazy, then my sweet Father intervened and took care of us in my naïve passion to trust Him.

Leave It!

Let me share from more recent times. Some years ago, God had called us to pastor a church in southern Oklahoma. Though we had endured some recent heartache from my previous pastorate, God had, once again, healed my heart and given me a new excitement to minister again. As always, I was excited about the new possibilities and the people we could see come to Christ.

As our kids were already grown and married by this time, we were empty-nesters and it was just Gretchen and me. While Gretchen was still working at her job in the Tulsa area, I went to the new town first and rented a small apartment. I moved a few of our things into the apartment and began my ministry at church. I settled into my new office and after new bookshelves were built, I unpacked my forty-five boxes of ministry books. For a pastor, these ministry books are our tools and a cherished resource. Some of these books had been given to me by my dad, by some of my cherished pastor friends who are now with the Lord, by other cherished friends and youth from our churches over the years, and from some of my favorite professors from Bible college and seminary who had become father figures in my life.

I also loved and enjoyed our staff at the church. They were good, dedicated people who became a big blessing in my life over those years. One of those special blessings was our youth pastor, Allen. Our hearts had immediately connected after beginning ministry together. Having spent my first twelve to fourteen years in youth ministry, a large part of my heart and passion was always pointed in that direction. He and I planned together, prayed together, cried together, witnessed together, and endured together.

God brought another blessing into our lives through the youth ministry there. A home for at-risk girls contacted Mark, a wonderful, loving friend in our church who is now with the Lord, asking for some help to make their Christmas brighter. He contacted our youth pastor and from that first contact with the girls at Christmas, a beautiful ministry was born.

These were teenage girls from very difficult backgrounds. The problems ran the gamut from all kinds of abuse, to drug addiction, to abandonment, to parents in prison or dead. We began to develop a relationship with the authorities there and let them know we were willing to help. Our youth leaders started signing them out and bringing them to fellowships with our youth ministry. We began to love them and share the gospel of Christ. God began to work in their lives in a powerful way and to show them a new direction in life. Though there was a negative reaction toward them by a few fearful people in the church, God continued changing lives. I can truly say that this was one of the most beautiful highlights of our time there as we watched these precious young ladies give their hearts to Christ and then follow the Lord in believer's baptism. They had many problems to deal with, but with Christ they had the One Who would carry them through it all.

Another of our special blessings also came through God's hand on the youth ministry there. God began to use some of our families in the church to take care of foreign exchange students while they were in our country. They became the host families for these students and made the commitment to receive them into their own homes and meet their needs. They began to bring these young people to church, and they became heavily involved in our youth ministry. This was a small church in a small town in Oklahoma, and God was sending us young people from all over the world. Just as with the teenage girls from the home, we began to love them and share the gospel with them. We treated them like our own kids with the love of Christ, and God used that to impact their lives in a powerful way. God gave us a divine appointment with kids from China, South Korea, Germany, and other countries. Most all of them gave their hearts to Christ while with us and followed the Lord in believer's baptism. It was a spectacle of God's grace and our hearts overflowed.

Some of the young families at the church also became a special blessing. We joined hearts as we served the Lord together in a host of events and ministry functions. They were so loving and supportive through every high and low that they became like my own kids. We walked through joy together, and we cried through sorrow together. Through the heartache and difficult times that any pastor goes through, they were always there trying to encourage us and to meet our needs. To this day, they are still a special part of our family.

A few months after we first arrived, Gretchen and I were seriously looking at different homes for sale. We looked at home after home, but there was always something that didn't quite fit. We happened to go to an open house one day without any expectations. We met a sweet Christian lady who was showing the house, and as we walked through it with her we knew it was the one. It was just what we were looking for, and she gave us a little information on the owners. They were an older couple who had to leave their home due to health issues and move into an assisted-living facility. We went to visit them at the facility and were overwhelmed by their sweet spirit and love. They were wonderful Christian people who were thrilled to have a pastor buying their home. We laughed and prayed with them for a while and as we were getting up to leave, the sweet lady asked her husband to go into the back room and get something. He came back out with a beautiful, expensive bed cover that had been custom made to match the drapes and carpet in one of the bedrooms. They handed it to us and told us they wanted us to have it for the home. The sweet gesture of generosity brought tears to my eyes, as I knew their journey on this earth was about over. This made our beautiful home even more special and confirmed that it was a gift from God. Not very long after that gesture of love, they went to their eternal home that was also custom decorated.

After a few years and some of the difficult struggles that all pastors walk through, my heart was burdened. I began to pray and seek God's direction for the future. I pondered what would happen now. We had some beautiful people in our lives whom we loved dearly, we were seeing some incredible things happen with young people coming to Christ, and even though it was not extravagant we had our beautiful home that we loved. From a human standpoint, we had more than ever before.

After months of desperate prayer and tears, I felt like God was telling me it was time to leave. Again, we faced another one of those defining moments. To leave the people we dearly loved, the amazing things God was doing in lives, the beautiful home we had grown to love, and the most generous salary we had received to date was one thing, but to leave everything with nothing to go to was something else. After all our years in ministry, I knew how things usually worked. When you feel like it's time to go, you begin to send out resumes and make contacts. You find an open door somewhere else and go talk to them. After you work through the details, find another church, and have everything confirmed and wrapped up, you then resign from your current church. That's the way it usually works.

After I shared with God in prayer that this was the way it was supposed to work, He told me, "This is not the way it is going to work for you." No, I didn't hear an audible voice. As Dr. Adrian Rogers used to say, "It was much louder than that!" I knew the choice was either to be obedient or disobedient. At that same time, I was about to go on another mission trip to the Philippines. I loved our mission work there and had always talked about wanting to do more. God was telling me that I would leave in order to be able to do more mission work. "Lord, there's no salary in my mission work," I responded. He said, "I am your salary." Here we were again at another faith-building, defining moment.

I graciously resigned from the church with no ministry, no job, and no clear direction about where to go. Our sweet friends lovingly surrounded us and prayed and worshiped with us over those next few months. God finally gave us His direction, so we sold the house and left. Little did I know when we left that I would be without a salary for two years. Was this that "unusual measure of trust in God beyond that exercised by most Christians"? Again, I don't know. I just know that God continues to stretch our faith and trust in Him even when it is very uncomfortable. Was it a lack of wisdom in not waiting until the Lord opened another door? All I can say is, when I hear the Lord's voice in my heart telling me to leave, my love for Him will not allow me to stay.

Enter It!

One of my most recent faith-building moments came just a few months ago in 2013. Some years ago in 2000, the Lord gave me an opportunity to join my dad and his Philippine mission work. He had started the mission work in the Philippines by faith in 1985 after spending several years working in the underground church behind the Iron Curtain. After his first trip to the Philippines with another mission leader, he launched out on his own to begin a new pioneering mission work. He went to the southern island of Mindanao in the Philippines and began sharing the gospel of Christ. Over a period of years, he established two mission bases on the island. Through his work there, the Lord has used him to build numerous churches, teach hundreds of pastors and leaders, start two seminaries, preach the gospel, and share desperately needed medicine with thousands. God has used him to impact untold lives for the cause of Christ.

He had asked me about going with him for years. As a busy pastor, I always found reasons not to go, but in 2000 the Lord laid it on my heart to join him. Without any expectations other than trying to love people and share the gospel I went. It was a very long and tiring trip of around thirty-eight hours from the time we left till we arrived at our first mission base.

When we arrived, I confess I was shocked by the shabby little Third-World airport. As we walked into the small, open-air baggage area, we were surrounded by many men who were aggressively begging us to let them carry our luggage. This was my first experience of seeing the desperation of people in a Third-World country. Making our way out to the parking lot through masses of people, Dad spotted his sweet friends who were there to pick us up. They loaded our luggage into an old, rickety jeepney[2] and we headed for the first mission base at their home.

With me being an American who had never been out of our country, everything was a shocking new experience. The shabby vehicles, the heartbreaking poverty, the shacks they lived in, and the terrible roads all served to place me into serious culture shock. However, there was also the most amazing contrast to all of this material poverty. When we arrived at their home, the only way I can describe the reception that day is that we were "swallowed up" with love. I had never seen anything quite like it. I was already on sensory overload and now this enveloping

---

[2] A long, truck-like vehicle converted from a jeep. Holds about thirty to forty people.

love added to the emotions I felt. Christ's love poured out of these people who had so little materially. I was stunned and overwhelmed from that day to this.

We spent a couple days preaching and teaching God's Word at a few conferences there. The next day we went out to some remote villages, shared the gospel, and then put our medicines out on tables and began to treat the people. On Sunday, we had the opportunity to preach at a local church Dad had started. I remember it was a pole-barn church[3] and leaned a few inches in one direction. I really thought it was about to fall down on everyone. On Monday morning, we got up early, loaded the jeepney, and headed out on the twelve-hour trip to the south mission base. This was another shocking experience. It was like riding in the back of an old, rickety pickup through a very bumpy pasture, while being nauseated for twelve hours.

When we arrived at the southern mission base, we were once again "swallowed up" with love. We followed the same routine as before spending a couple days preaching and teaching at the conferences and then driving out to some remote villages to share the gospel and medicine. By this time, my emotional cup was running over. We were about to take the long trip back home and as we said goodbye, they cried and gave us little gifts. I truly felt these people were part of my family after only a few short days.

After we got back home and I went back to my pastor's study at the church, I had a hard time concentrating. In one sense, my heart was still in the Philippines. God had so imprinted my heart with the people and the mission work there that I didn't know if I could continue to pastor. I continued to pray and struggle through the coming weeks and months. I realized one day that God had placed a call on my life to minister to the people in the Philippines. I knew then that even though I would continue to pastor, I would lead teams back to the Philippines each year. From that time until now, I have followed that call of God, and He has continued to do miraculous things.

For the last thirteen years, I have poured my heart into our precious people there and as I write this am preparing our next mission team to go back in a few months. Though I am not shocked (usually) anymore by the things I see there, it is no less heartbreaking to see the desperate needs. Our families, crews, and people in both locations are

---

[3] A makeshift church put together with a few support poles and a roof.

one of the treasures of my heart. To hear the little ones running out to greet us and shouting, "Daddy Mark, Daddy Mark!" and knowing that God is using me to bless them is something I have no words to express. If any of you in the Philippines ever get to read this, I want you to know you are one of the biggest blessings in my life, and I love you very much!

On our most recent mission trip a few months ago in 2013, God once again touched many lives. Our American pastors, Steve and Lester, trained and encouraged the pastors and leaders there. Our nurse, Dana, taught and encouraged the women. Our photographer, Amanda, taught and encouraged everyone. Our youth minister, Jared, discipled and encouraged the youth, and I challenged and encouraged our college group called "Champions for Christ." We also had the opportunity to share the gospel of Christ at a public high school in which many of the students made a commitment of their lives to Christ. Again, it was a life-altering experience. I came home with my heart full.

As we were trying to fly out of the Philippines to come home, we encountered a problem. When we arrived at the airport and tried to check in we found out that our flight had been canceled. We knew from some weather reports that a terrible storm was hitting the Philippines just north of us. It was actually hitting some of the islands, at the same time we were at the airport, and blocking our flight path back to Manila. It was super Typhoon Yolanda with the highest recorded winds on record. Only through an intervention of God were we able to scramble and get another flight. After two weeks of tiring ministry and the long flights home, I was completely drained and even felt sick. I got home and crashed. I just needed some recovery time.

The next day I began to see the terrible news reports coming out of the city of Tacloban on the island of Leyte in the Philippines just north of where our mission work was located on Mindanao. It was a complete disaster area. It reminded me of the destruction I saw with our mission teams in Port-au-Prince, Haiti, after the mega earthquake destroyed the city. The destruction in Tacloban was unbelievable because they had not only had tornado-force winds but the added destruction of a twenty- to twenty-five-foot storm surge (like a tidal wave) that had engulfed the city. The pictures were shocking and the death toll was rising. I prayed for them and thought about a way I could send some money to help.

That same day as I watched the shocking news reports I got a call. It was a friend of mine who was, and still is, the president of an international relief organization. I had served with him before, and he knew of my long-term mission work in the Philippines. He asked me if I had seen the news reports and what I was going to do about it. Having just returned tired and sick from my own mission work the day before, I told him that my heart was certainly there, but I didn't have the money to go back. His response was, "Then you need to start packing your bags." He told me he would raise the money but that I needed to go back immediately as soon as we could get a flight. That set everything in motion and after some scrambling and financial help from my church, I stepped back on a plane a few days later. I want you to see the raw, untouched thoughts that were running through my head. This is what I posted on Facebook.

When your faith is SLAPPED in the face.

It is one of the most devastated places on the planet right now. The typhoon in the Philippines was one of the most powerful ever recorded with tornado-force winds. There was a 20 to 25-foot storm surge that covered virtually everything, leaving a path of destruction that looks otherworldly. Thousands are laying everywhere dead. Tens of thousands are starving and without water or any kind of medical help or shelter. There is looting, stealing, and desperation just to survive. To say that it is a terrible tragedy is a terrible understatement.

O.K. I feel terrible for those poor people, but that is halfway around the world. I will pray for them. Then the Lord gives me one of those, "I am calling you to go" kind of moments. This is when faith is slapped in the face. To be honest, I just returned from two weeks in the Philippines and I am exhausted and my stomach is still messed up. I usually take a couple weeks just to get back to normal, but the day after I return the Lord puts it in front of me to jump back on a plane quickly.

Not to return to my normal mission work there where I have a ministry family after 13 years, but to something I have not known. This is when faith is slapped in the face. I am going to a place I have never been with people I have never known. This is a place that is devastated on such a scale that it dwarfs me. I don't know how we will get to the island. I don't know how we will be able to travel. I don't know if the pastors I will look for are dead or alive. I don't know where we will sleep. I don't know how we will get back out. I don't even know about food or water. This is when faith is slapped in the face.

That was definitely one of those faith-building, defining moments though another one that was even more intense was coming soon.

I had already contacted my trusted Filipino partner and dear friend Rudy to meet me on an adjoining island. I knew I would need him to help me walk through the maze of problems we were about to encounter. Rudy had been with me from the beginning of my mission work and became one of my dearest brothers in Christ. He was not only great at dealing with people, but he was also retired military, which made him even more valuable in dealing with security issues.

I had left early on a Wednesday morning from Tulsa. I flew through Seoul, South Korea, and on to the Philippines still tired and sick to my stomach. I was just walking by faith and asking the Lord to give me the strength I needed. I had coordinated with Rudy so that his flight would arrive before mine and he would be waiting on me. When I arrived at the airport on the neighboring island of Cebu and made it through the processing station I did not see Rudy. With an uneasy feeling in my heart, I texted Ever, his wife, to ask where he was, and she told me his flight from Mindanao to Cebu had been canceled. She told me he had to take the boat. I thought, *Oh great, he is on the slow boat!* This was exactly what I wanted to avoid. I didn't want to arrive at a foreign airport in the middle of the night feeling sick with no one to help me navigate. She told me he would not be there until the next morning around 6:30 to 7:00 a.m. After an attempt to find a hotel with a taxi driver I couldn't understand and who charged three times the normal fare, I went back to the airport and slept on the crowded airport floor in the back hall. All the seats and part of the floor were filled with Filipinos sleeping and waiting on flights. This was the first challenge of many to come and the news got worse the next morning.

After trying to rest with one eye open on the airport floor that night, the morning light began to shine through the windows. I was very relieved when I got a text message from Rudy that he had arrived at the airport. I immediately got up, grabbed my backpack, and went looking for him. After walking through a couple crowded terminals, I saw his smiling face. With great joy we hugged and greeted each other. We found a little coffee shop and sat down to enjoy some breakfast, not knowing when we might be able to eat again. I started talking about making plans to get to the devastated city of Tacloban and helping some of the people there.

In talking about how we might get to Tacloban, Rudy had a troubled look on his face. As he began to speak, my heart sank and thoughts of fear began to circle around me like vultures. Rudy spoke to me in a very serious tone and told me that all of my most-trusted pastor friends and leaders from Mindanao had said, "Do not go to Tacloban!" They were unanimous. They said, "You will be mobbed and robbed by the desperate people there." We had already heard reports that other relief workers going in before us had already been mobbed. I suddenly felt that fear was attempting to overwhelm my heart and stop this mission work.

Rudy shared another bit of stunning information. As the storm surge was rushing into the city, the authorities at the city jail panicked and opened all the jail doors. In addition to the destruction and chaos of the storm, there were now around a thousand criminals loose in the city. Here I was again at another one of those faith-building, defining moments. This was a gut check moment when you have to decide whether the faith you've talked about is real or just words. I will be honest; it was an intense moment with intense feelings for me. We had no contacts to meet us after many calls, e-mails, texts, and Facebook messages. We would have to sleep wherever we could on the street, in a devastated building or under a piece of tin. We would sleep and work in whatever weather in a desperate and hostile environment. At this point, it all seemed very dangerous with all the reports and all of my best friends telling me not to go. I got very emotional and told Rudy, "I can't not go! I've been sent here, and people have given money to help those devastated by the super typhoon." We sat there quietly for a moment with tears in our eyes. What happened next was one of those God moments.

We decided we would try to get some help from our American military when we arrived. If that didn't work, we would try to find some local police if they had survived and were willing to help. We were feverishly trying to text and call every contact in the Tacloban area we had been given by my Philippine pastor friends. We didn't get a single response. We needed a contact in the worst way and could not get anyone. We believed the super typhoon had knocked out all communications, and no one was able to call or communicate with us. Though struggling inside, I looked at Rudy and said, "God sent us here, and I believe He will make a way." We were both emotional and agreed together that we trusted God to make a way. I must share a personal note. When you have a friend who will walk into that kind of dangerous environment with you, you have someone who truly loves you. Rudy was willing to walk with me into whatever danger we would face. I will always love him for that kind of heart.

With all of the intensity of the moment upon us, something amazing happened. Just minutes later, Rudy got a call from Pastor Rayos right in the city of Tacloban. I saw the smile on Rudy's face as he listened. After the phone call ended, we looked directly at each other and laughed with joy at the miracle contact, not thinking anyone could even call from there. The relief and gratitude to God filled our hearts. Pastor Rayos had told us to come, and he would pick us up at the airport. How he would pick us up in that complete devastation with no fuel available we didn't know, but we were filled with joy. We booked a commercial flight from Cebu to Tacloban and after numerous delays for hours due to storm complications, we flew to the devastated city. From the air we were able to see some of the coastal areas wiped away. When we got off the plane the sights were shocking. The airport was in shambles. The scene looked like a tornado came through with the addition of a twenty-five-foot tidal wave. It was complete destruction with very little left standing.

As we walked out of the devastated airport and through the gates with armed guards, we began to look for Pastor Rayos. After a few uneasy minutes of walking through groups of people in what was left of the parking lot we found him. He was our divine contact from God, and we were very glad to see him. He and his driver Bob took us (after buying fuel in Coke bottles off the street) to the inner part of the city to New Life Baptist Church. We spent nine days with these precious brothers and sisters in Christ trying to buy some relief supplies and minister to the devastated people there. It was difficult to see the devastation and death all around us, but it was also glorious to see the light of Christ shining through these people in the midst of tragedy. Pastor Rayos, his wife, Jan, and the New Life family actually ministered to us. At the end of our stay, as we looked at the long lines and chaos at the airport, it seemed impossible we would get out on a commercial flight from that devastated airport. God miraculously provided. We talked to our American military guys at the airport and were able to fly out on a big C-130 military transport plane. What a difficult and blessed time it was!

So, was it faith or foolishness? I had everybody I knew and loved from that culture telling me not to go. I knew it was very possible we could be mobbed and have our supplies stolen, as every store in the city had been looted with starving, thirsty people everywhere. After hearing about a thousand criminals running around the city, I had even thought it was possible we could be killed. Was this evidence of the gift of faith that is "an unusual measure of trust in God beyond that exercised by most Christians"? I believe it was by God's grace, even though I saw many American relief workers walking off the planes on the tarmac that day and also many great Filipino doctors who stayed with us at the church and met the needs of hundreds of hurting people. Maybe all those courageous believers had that gift of faith. Our loving and gracious God called us and provided for us to obey that call. What some would call faith others might call stupidity or careless impulse. You can make up your own mind. I think you can guess what my answer would be.

As I look back now over my journey of forty years with the Lord, I have a better view of the big picture. Looking at these experiences God has placed in my life, of which I have only shared a few, it confirms His gifting and provision. Whether it was a Sunday morning in church when God spoke to my heart to write a check for everything in the checking account, or His call to go on a forty-day fast, or His call a few weeks ago to give away everything I had saved for our upcoming mission trip, or even His direction to walk into a home to help someone writhing around with a demonic problem, He has always been faithful and has always provided. It is only because of His grace gifts in my life that I can do anything of spiritual value. He is my source! He is my life! Any grace gifts we have just shout His glory.

I pray for you as you search the scripture and see what God is doing in and through your life that you would use whatever spiritual gifts God has given you to edify and build up the Body of Christ. I pray that you would invest your life and gifts to impact as many lives as possible with the life-changing love of Jesus Christ. As you are faithful to follow God's will and Word through the experiences of your life, I think you will also see a beautiful pattern emerge that will reveal God's design. You will realize something that God has been preparing you for and leading you to. Some of it you may see in the short term and some may be in the long term. You will see His gifts and His purpose. I pray that you will live to impact eternity. "Now to Him who is able to do exceedingly abundantly above all that we ask or think, according to the power that works in us, to Him be glory in the church by Christ Jesus to all generations, forever and ever. Amen" (Ephesians 3:20–21).

Heart Healer

You've gone so long you don't recall
that time before you took the fall
And pain became your constant friend,
the heartbreak that has had no end

But One Who walked the road before
has felt that pain and so much more
He's reaching down to dry your tears
to heal your heart and take your fears

The words were said, they tore your heart,
your long-held trust just torn apart
Your life will never be the same,
all plans are burned and fear's aflame

Yet even in your darkest hour,
you're not beyond His strength and power
The One Who spoke and there was light
is touching you to bring new sight

The hand that took the nails for you
can touch your heart and make it new
Though you lost hope, He never will,
He paid for hope on Calvary's hill

If He can heal a blind man's eyes
and hang each star up in the skies
Then He can heal your broken heart,
restore and mend each shattered part.

May 2007

Final Note

Her name was Bernice. She was smiling when I met her one day in her nursing home room. I was pastoring a church and had gone to the nursing home to visit some other friends. A deacon from church had mentioned her and told me what a blessing she had been to him as he ministered there.

As I walked into her room, the light of Christ on her face and in her life was evident. I sat down and began to talk with Bernice, thinking I would try to be an encouragement to her. Though her spirit was bright and full of life, her body was not. With numerous health issues that came from many years on this earth, she now rarely even made it out of her room. She was in one little room at the end of one of several halls. This secluded little spot unknown to all but some family and a few friends was where she would live out the rest of her limited days.

As we began to talk, I realized this was different than most of my visits to the nursing home. This was not a sweet soul just waiting to die. She still had a purpose in life, though most would wonder what that could possibly be in a little secluded room at the end of the hall in a nursing home. She began to tell me about her ministry for the Lord. She had previously been a member of our church years before but had moved to another church family afterward. She sat in her little chair by the end table with a light and her Bible, and she explained her daily ministry. After her time in the Word each morning, she would enter into a time of intercessory prayer. She would take her pastor's picture out of her Bible, lay it on top of her Bible, and lay her hand on top of his picture. She would then begin to intercede for her pastor and call on the Lord for blessing, healing, strength, wisdom, and favor on his life. I was humbled in her presence as I saw a prayer warrior that would not give up. I was also convicted, as I had wanted to give up recently.

She then told me something that has impacted me to this day. She said that when she heard from our mutual friend that I had come to pastor her old church, she began to call out my name to the Lord each day and intercede for me also. I was stunned by the compassion and ministry of this little old lady. Her spiritual strength and heart for ministry put me to shame. She told me that she needed my picture so that she could put her hand on it each day and call out to the Lord the same way she did for her own pastor. There were tears in my eyes then as there are now many years later as I write. I took her a picture a few days later.

I can't tell you what it meant to a struggling pastor to know that a sweet prayer warrior in a little room at the end of a long hall was putting her frail hand on my picture each day and calling out to the Lord for me. That is a hero of the faith! I can say in all honesty that I believe her spiritual ministry known only to God and a few others had as much or more impact in the kingdom as anything I was doing. When most of the sweet people I visited there had given up and were settled into the waiting and enduring mode, she was using her spiritual gift to make an eternal impact.

I don't know what other gifts Bernice may have had, but I believe she definitely had the gift of helps. She had become a burden bearer with me as I struggled through some difficult times. I didn't get to see her a lot, but it was always a desire of mine when I was out visiting to go to that little room at the end of the long hall and see the sweet prayer warrior who was daily lifting me up to the throne in prayer. There are a few of those moments in life when you know you have had the privilege of being in the presence of someone with which God gave you a divine appointment. She was one of them for me.

Maybe you feel like you are at the end of a long hall in a little room and have very little to give. You know Christ personally and walk with Him but feel like you have little worth in kingdom work. Let me assure you that just as God used Bernice to impact my life and many others, He has gifted you to make an eternal difference. Whether your spiritual gift is more evident to others or known to almost no one, it is known by our Almighty God on the throne. He is not done with you yet! You can make a difference, and when we get to glory I believe that many, like Bernice and maybe you also, will have more rewards than pastors like me. You can lay up treasures in heaven and impact kingdom work no matter what your situation may be. Lord, I pray that whoever reads this book will have your blessing, healing, strength, wisdom, and favor on his or her life as they love and serve you! Amen!

My Anchor

When darkened clouds surround my soul
When hurt and pain around me roll
Whatever come my lot may be
His loving hand still anchors me

When words have cut me like a knife
When hatred causes bitter strife
Whatever come my lot may be
His loving hand still anchors me

When sickness tears my loved ones down
When death's cold stare has come around
Whatever come my lot may be
His loving hand still anchors me

When purpose fades and questions rise
And burning tears have filled my eyes
Whatever come my lot may be
His loving hand still anchors me

When those we love have gone astray
Have broken our hearts and saddened our day
Whatever come my lot may be
His loving hand still anchors me

Whatever the storms, whatever the gales
Whatever pain blows against my sails
Though battered and torn my boat may be
His loving hand still anchors me.

December 2001

Final Question

As I conclude this book, I have one final concern for you. I have prayed over this book that the Lord would use it as a blessing to those who read it and are seeking spiritual truth. So, if you have read this book, I have prayed for you. Wherever you might stand on the spiritual gifts and their use, my heart's desire is for you to truly know Christ personally and be secure in Him.

So please allow me to ask a final question. Is it possible that you are where I was spiritually? I had prayed the sinner's prayer, been baptized by immersion, became a member of a church, had gone to Sunday school and church every time the doors were open, went to Vacation Bible School, prayer meetings on Wednesday nights, and had tried my best to live like a Christian. If you would have asked me if I was a Christian I would have immediately said yes and pointed to the things I had done. I probably would have been a little insulted if you had asked. Please forgive me if you are a little insulted by my question.

My problem was that I was following a religious system and placing my trust in the things I had done and was continuing to do. I finally realized that something was very wrong in my heart. I heard about being a new creation in Christ, but it was just nice words to me at the time. It was religious speech. I cried out to God asking what was wrong with me. I was churning inside. The Holy Spirit spoke to my heart and revealed that I was a Christian in name only. I realized that I had never been changed on the inside. I had gone through the motions of being a Christian. Even though I had assumed all those years that I was saved because of the prayer and other religious actions, I was just acting out a role.

When the Holy Spirit convicted my heart and revealed my need to move beyond religion and into a personal relationship with Christ, I responded with everything that was in me. I was tired of the empty words and the emptiness in my soul. I erupted in prayer and poured my heart out to God. I had heard the words before, but now they made sense. I knew I had sinned. "For all have sinned and fall short of the glory of God" (Romans 3:23). I knew what would happen if I continued in that direction. It was clear to me as I wept in that little room by myself that Christ was changing me from the inside out. "For the wages of sin is death, but the gift of God is eternal life in Christ Jesus our Lord" (Romans 6:23). I realized God's incredible love for me and the price that Jesus paid. "For God so loved the world [that is you and me] that He gave His only begotten Son, that whoever believes [trusts in, relies completely upon, clings to] in Him should not perish but have everlasting life" (John 3:16).

I remember surrendering everything to Christ that day and making a blank check commitment of my life to Him. I turned away from my works-based, messed-up life and turned it all over to Him. I asked Him to come into my life as my personal Savior and Lord. I thanked Him for dying on the cross and shedding His blood for my sins. I praised Him that He rose from the dead. I thanked Him for coming to live within me. This was a genuine surrender from the bottom of my heart. That was the moment I was changed on the inside. I remember the next day being surprised at how my motives and desires had changed. Though I had a bunch of growing to do, I had been changed and I knew it.

If you find yourself where I was and sense the Holy Spirit prompting your heart now, just give it all to Him. This is your moment. You don't have to be in a church service to do it. Move from the religious system into a real, personal relationship with Christ. Surrender your heart and life to Him. Don't worry about what others may think even if you have been in church or called yourself a Christian. Your salvation and eternal life is infinitely more important than embarrassment or what others might think. Just pour your heart out to God and surrender your life to Him right now. There is no exact formula of words, but if you need a little help you could pray, "Dear Lord, I know I am a sinner, and I can't save myself. I thank You that You died on the cross to pay for my sins, that You were buried and rose again. I turn away from this direction my life is headed and surrender my heart and life to You. Please forgive me of my sins and save me and come into my life as my Lord and Savior. In Jesus' name I pray. Amen!"

Remember, just saying those words will not save you. That was my mistake early in life. There is no exact formula of words, and your trust cannot be in the words; it must be completely in the Lord Jesus. The real inner change comes when the Holy Spirit is convicting your heart of your need and you genuinely surrender your life to Jesus. When you change direction and make that complete surrender of your life to Jesus, you will become a new creation in Christ. Your life will be changed forever, and we will meet someday. God bless you as you fulfill His purpose for your life. "For we are God's masterpiece. He has created us anew in Christ Jesus, so that we can do the good things He planned for us long ago" (Ephesians 2:10, NLT).

Scripture References

Preface
John 16:13
2 Timothy 3:16–17

Chapter 1
2 Peter 1:2–4
1 Corinthians 12:12–13
Ephesians 1:3
Luke 11:11–13
Colossians 2:9–10
Philippians 4:13
John 16:13
Romans 8:26
Philippians 4:19
1 John 5:14–15

Chapter 2
Ephesians 5:17–18
Galatians 5:22–23
Galatians 5:16
Ephesians 6:17
Philippians 4:13
Romans 8:1
Colossians 2:13–14
Acts 1:4–5
Luke 24:49
John 7:37–39
Acts 15:7–9
1 Corinthians 12:13
Acts 1:8
Acts 2:2–4
John 14:16–17

Ephesians 6:16
1 Corinthians 12:13
2 Corinthians 5:17
Romans 8:9
John 13:34–35

Chapter 3
Isaiah 66:3
Matthew 24:27
John 14:6
2 Timothy 2:15
John 8:31–32
Matthew 27:5
Luke 10:37
1 Corinthians 15:29

Chapter 4
1 Corinthians 6:9–11
1 Corinthians 3:1–3
John 10:10
2 Corinthians 11:13–15
1 Corinthians 14:19
Revelation 22:18–19

Chapter 5
1 Peter 5:5
Philippians 2:2–4
James 1:27

Chapter 6
John 13:3–35

Chapter 6 continued
1 Corinthians 6:19–20
Galatians 2:20
2 Corinthians 5:17
Galatians 5:16–17
Romans 13:14
1 Corinthians 3:1–3
1 Corinthians 13:1
2 Corinthians 12:4
1 Corinthians 3:1–3a
1 Corinthians 13:2
Hebrews 10:24
1 Corinthians 1:11–13
Hebrews 12:1–2

Chapter 7
1 Corinthians 5:1
1 Corinthians 5:6
1 Corinthians 14:19
1 Corinthians 14:40
1 Corinthians 14:2
John 1:11
Acts 2:5
1 Corinthians 14:29
2 Timothy 3:16–17

Chapter 9
Ephesians 3:20–21

Final Question
Romans 3:23
Romans 6:23
John 3:16
Ephesians 2:10

Bibliography

Barnes, Albert. *Barnes Notes on the New Testament: II Cor.–Gal.* Edited by Robert Frew. Grand Rapids, Michigan: Baker Book House, 1965.

Brooks, Keith L. *The Summarized Bible.* Grand Rapids, Michigan: Baker Book House, 1975.

Criswell, W. A. *The Holy Spirit in Today's World.* Grand Rapids, Michigan: Zondervan Publishing House, 1966.

Criswell, W. A., ed. *The Criswell Study Bible.* With the assistance of Paige Patterson, Mallory Chamberlin, Dorothy Kelley Patterson, and Jack Pogue. Nashville, Tennessee: Thomas Nelson Publishers, 1979.

Dennis, Lane T., Wayne Grudem, J. I. Packer, C. John Collins, Thomas R. Schreiner, and Justin Taylor, eds. With the assistance of Barry J. Beitzel, Leen Ritmeyer, John Currid, David W. Chapman, and Travis Buchanan. *The English Standard Version Study Bible.* Wheaton, Illinois: Crossway, 2008.

Gardiner, George E. *The Corinthian Catastrophe.* Grand Rapids, Michigan: Kregel Publications, 1974.

MacArthur, John. *The MacArthur Study Bible.* Nashville, Tennessee: Word Publishing, 1997.

MacArthur, John F., Jr. *Charismatic Chaos.* Grand Rapids, Michigan: Zondervan Publishing House, 1992.

McHenry, Raymond. *McHenry's Stories for the Soul.* Peabody, Massachusetts: Hendrickson Publishers, 2001.

Packer, J. I., Merrill C. Tenney, and William White Jr., eds. *Nelson's Illustrated Encyclopedia of Bible Facts.* Nashville, Tennessee: Thomas Nelson Publishers, 1995.

Patterson, Paige. *The Troubled Triumphant Church.* Dallas, Texas: Criswell Publications, 1983.

Radmacher, Earl D., ed. With the assistance of Ronald B. Allen and H. Wayne House. *The Nelson Study Bible*. Nashville, Tennessee: Thomas Nelson Publishers, 1997.

Robertson, A. T. *Word Pictures in the New Testament*. Nashville, Tennessee: Broadman Press, 1931.

Unger, Merrill F. *The New Unger's Bible Dictionary*. Edited by R. K. Harrison. With the assistance of Howard F. Vos and Cyril J. Barber. Chicago, Illinois: Moody Press, 1988.

Unger, Merrill F. *The New Unger's Bible Handbook*. Revised by Gary Larson. Chicago, Illinois: Moody Press, 1984.

Vincent, Marvin R. *Word Studies in the New Testament*. Grand Rapids, Michigan: Wm. B. Eerdmans Publishing Co., 1985.

Vine, W. E. *An Expository Dictionary of New Testament Words*. Old Tappan, New Jersey: Fleming H. Revell Company, 1966.

Vines, Jerry. *Spirit Works*. Nashville, Tennessee: Broadman & Holman Publishers, 1999.

Walvoord, John F. *The Holy Spirit*. Findlay, Ohio: Dunham Publishing Company, 1958.

Walvoord, John F. and Roy B. Zuck, eds. *The Bible Knowledge Commentary*. With the assistance of Kenneth L. Barber, Eugene H. Merrill, and Stanley D. Toussaint. Wheaton, Illinois: SP Publications, Inc., 1983.

Wiersbe, Warren W. *Be Wise*. Wheaton, Illinois: Victor Books a division of SP Publications, Inc., 1985.

Witty, Robert G. *Holy Spirit Power*. Jacksonville, Florida: Pioneer Press, 1966.

Woolf, Henry Bosley, ed. *Webster's New Collegiate Dictionary*. With the assistance of Edward Artin, F. Stuart Crawford, E. Ward Gilman, Mairé Weir Kay, and Roger W. Pease, Jr. Springfield, Massachusetts: G. & C. Merriam Company, 1981.

Zodhiates, Spiros. *Tongues?*. Chattanooga, Tennessee: AMG Publishers, 1983.

This book is available for purchase in hardback, paperback, and eBook editions through innovopublishing.com or your favorite online retailer.

ABOUT INNOVO PUBLISHING

Innovo Publishing is a full-service Christian publisher serving the Christian and wholesome markets. Innovo creates, distributes, and markets quality hardback and paperback books, eBooks (Kindle, Nook, iPhone, iPad, ePub), audiobooks, music (CDs and MP3s), and film through traditional publishing, cooperative publishing, and independent publishing models. Innovo provides distribution, marketing, and automated order fulfillment through a network of thousands of physical and online wholesalers, retailers, bookstores, music stores, schools, and libraries worldwide. Visit Innovo at www.innovopublishing.com.

FOR A HIGHER PURPOSE

"In this publishing experience I have found Innovo Publishing to be not only outstanding professionals, but also solid conservative Christians that have a great commitment to sharing Christ and the truths of God's Word. Their process is very thorough in order to produce the highest quality books. They have answered every question with honesty and integrity and have given experienced guidance through every facet of my work. They have become trusted advisors and friends and I would highly recommend them to other authors." —Mark D. Hyskell, Author